Einstein
and
Dostoyevsky

BORIS KUZNETSOV

Chairman of the International Einstein Committee

Translated from the Russian by
Vladimir Talmy

HUTCHINSON EDUCATIONAL

HUTCHINSON EDUCATIONAL LTD
3 Fitzroy Square, London W1

London Melbourne Sydney Auckland
Wellington Johannesburg Cape Town
and agencies throughout the world

First published in Great Britain May 1972

C

*This book has been set in Baskerville type, printed in Great Britain
on smooth wove paper by Anchor Press, and
bound by Wm. Brendon, both of Tiptree, Essex*

ISBN 0 09 106660 3

Einstein and Dostoyevsky

Contents

I

Experimental Realism

Any attempt to analyse Einstein's remarks about Dostoyev-sky—for instance 'He gives me more than any thinker, more than Gauss'—inevitably raises those more general problems which, however much they may be modified in the cultural progress of man, constantly recur. These are the problems of cognition and action, thought and experience, truth and goodness, the harmony and disharmony of the world. Though they are as old as civilisation itself, we shall, in this book, concern ourselves with the past three centuries only.

The seventeenth century had to answer the question posed to it by Hamlet. In the soul of the Prince of Denmark the old, medieval ideal of logically sound, scholastic thinking was being replaced, with tragic consequences, by a new ideal: thought must engender action, must be nurtured by action and find embodiment in action. Science responded with the experimental method and, a century later, with the industrial revolution. Public thinking responded two centuries later in the Jacobinic dictatorship. In the seventeenth century reason was busy building up a line of departure for the coming offensive. Galileo discovered, in the concept of free motion that continues indefinitely and requires no sustaining force, a basis for a new scheme of reality. Instead of the Aristotelian scheme of 'natural' places, the scheme of uniform motions provided an explanation of the harmony of the universe. Descartes enlarged on the concept of inertia by ascribing conservation of velocity to bodies moving in a straight line. He developed a physics in which there was nothing but moving matter. Spinoza gave this physics a universal outlook, rejecting Descartes' *res extensa*, or extended substance. Finally Newton, who made mechanics axiomatic by introducing the concept of force and enunciated the law of universal gravity, rounded off the first circle in the development of a rational scheme of the universe. He assumed the possibility of a body being acted upon not only by other bodies, but by space itself. This was to some extent a departure from the classical ideal of science. None the less, the scientific picture of the world acquired unequivocal authenticity, as the quantitative relationships of classical mechanics were susceptible of experimental verification.

The eighteenth century saw the advance of rationalism. It was called the Age of Reason, and it *was* an age of reason, which claimed the absolute accuracy of all its conclusions and their universal applicability to both the macrocosm and the microcosm. In those days men thought that a logical development of Newtonian mechanics could explain the totality of natural phenomena, that a knowledge of the co-ordinates and velocities of all the molecules of the universe was sufficient to predict the whole of its future history to any degree of accuracy. They also thought that the logical construction of concepts would enable them to devise a scheme for a harmonious social order, and this hope inspired Babeuf and, before him, its pre-revolutionary adherents.

In the nineteenth century men realised that reality could be cognised and transformed only through the rejection of immutable forms, universal mathematical relationships and petrified logical laws. Though, as Laplace said, it was easier for reason to forge ahead than to delve into itself, the delving proved inevitable. Goethe pointed out that reality could not be reduced to logical schemes ('Theory, my friend, is grey, but eternally green is the tree of life'). German classical philosophy discovered that unless it changed its basic axioms it was brought to a halt by serious and insoluble contradictions. Then classical philosophy reached an important conclusion: thought obtains infinite power when it becomes plastic and alive, when it is not constrained by absolutes of any kind. Carnot, Clausius, and, towards the end of the century, Boltzmann demonstrated that the laws of behaviour of large populations of molecules are of an entirely different nature from the laws governing the behaviour of individual molecules. The former are statistical, and make natural processes irreversible; the latter fit into the framework of the mechanics of reversible processes. Analogously, Darwin discovered the statistical laws of evolution: environment affects the fate of a species, a statistical aggregate, and only the *probability* of various individual fates. Lobachevsky, and later Riemann, arrived at the idea of two mutually exclusive systems of geometry: Euclidean (in which the sum of the angles of a triangle equals two right angles; it is possible to draw only one line parallel to another through a point outside the latter; perpendiculars to a straight line are parallel, etc.) and non-Euclidean (in which the sum of the angles of a triangle is either less or more than two right angles; it is possible to draw an infinite number of lines parallel to another, or none at all, through a point; perpendiculars to a straight line either diverge or converge, etc.). The correspondence of these geometries to reality depended on the physical processes and dimensions of the domain in

9

which they were considered. Very soon the term 'non-Euclidean' was used to define not only mathematically paradoxical systems but also any conceptions rejecting axioms that were once regarded as unshakable.

Nineteenth-century social thought arrived at the revolutionary conclusion that social harmony could be achieved on the ruins of institutes that had seemed logically as sound and impregnable as Euclid's axioms. Here, however, the analogy ends. The social harmony which the leading revolutionary thinkers of the nineteenth century contemplated differed from the cosmic harmony envisaged by the most revolutionary mathematicians, astronomers and physicists of the age. Lobachevsky and Riemann thought it possible to abandon Euclidean relationships in immense cosmic domains. The cosmic harmony, even non-Euclidean, was nevertheless cosmic, undisturbed by microscopic processes, ruling over statistically averaged processes in which the fate of a speck of dust was as immaterial to the motion of a planet as the fate of a single organism was to the life or death of the species. Social harmony, on the other hand, is based on the liberation of man from the dominion of the elemental forces that govern statistically averaged quantities. A harmonious social system must ensure the happiness of *every* individual. Here the 'geometry' of the whole is based not on ignoring its microscopic parts but, on the contrary, on due consideration for every single one of them.

Dostoyevsky's main philosophical novels—*Crime and Punishment, The Idiot, The Possessed, The Raw Youth, The Brothers Karamazov*—were written in the decade and a half between 1866 and 1880. They left mankind older, though at first unable to analyse what had actually happened. 'The earth is saturated with human tears from crust to centre' is the primary motif of Dostoyevsky's novels. This is not a conclusion drawn from statistical tables. Quite the reverse. Nor is it an ill-founded and personal impression, for it is not a question of individuals alone, but of mankind as a whole. Mankind, however, exists in every individual, and social and moral problems unfold within the framework of a literary hero's psychology, in the shape of *aesthetic* generalisations. The conclusion of rationalist thinking—that cosmic harmony is unacceptable if it ignores the fate of the in-individual—is only valid in the context of an aesthetic generalisation which admits the unique and sovereign value of the individual character.

The culminating point of *The Brothers Karamazov* is the scene in the inn where Ivan Karamazov talks to his brother Alyosha and rejects the providential harmony of a universe which is unable to avenge the sufferings of a single 'small' man. Whatever the 'macroscopic' harmony of the whole, a mother cannot forgive the sufferings of her tortured child. And if that is so, Ivan Karamazov says, what becomes of the harmony? ' "Is there in the whole world a being who could or would have the right to forgive? I don't want harmony. I don't want it, out of the love I bear to mankind. . . . Besides, too high a price has been placed on harmony. We cannot afford to pay so much for admission. And therefore I hasten to return my ticket of admission." '[1]

The chapter in which Ivan Karamazov 'returns his ticket of admission' is called 'Rebellion'. It is not only the culminating point of the novel but even perhaps the culmination of all Dostoyevsky's work. It is the most piercing note in that craving for harmony which has distinguished the history of human culture and which remains as a question addressed to the twentieth century. This craving is of the same

[1] Fyodor Dostoyevsky, *The Brothers Karamazov*, translated by David Magarshack (Folio Society, 1964), p. 257.

order as the scientific discoveries of the nineteenth century, which also posed questions to the future. It is their emotional, psychological and aesthetic equivalent. Human life is torn with disharmony, and the earth runs with human blood and tears. Harmony can only be 'non-Euclidean', paradoxical and closed to traditional 'Euclidean' thinking. But across its path lies a grave predicament: the moral intuition of man rejects a harmony of the universe that is based on disregard even for a single localised, comparatively microscopic act of disharmony, of disregard even for the tears of an unhappy child.

Whatever one may think of Dostoyevsky's public views, however erroneous or reactionary his political and social ideas may have been, the essence of his art is an appeal addressed to the twentieth century; man needs a social and moral harmony that does not ignore local disharmonies and that refuses to accept the individual sufferings of any man, a harmony that leaves no place for coercion, oppression or contempt for the weak.

This appeal could not be expressed in any abstract or statistically descriptive form, for it involves a protest against disregard of the individual. Such a protest is only significant within the framework of an aesthetic generalisation, in the form of specific literary characters. We shall soon see that Dostoyevsky's remarkable ability to create authentic characters affected the intellectual content of his books.

Dostoyevsky came of a different social stratum from the other great Russian writers of his generation. Born in the wing of a hospital for the poor, where his father worked as a doctor, Dostoyevsky had no memories of avenues of centenarian lime trees such as figure so frequently in the novels of writers of gentry stock. For him there were no family traditions, no stable family life, no familiar surroundings to be remembered. Turgenev's and Tolstoy's heroes, like their authors, have experienced the natural harmony associated with a family estate, with all its rural beauty and domestic comfort. The confusion and disharmony of their souls stands in contrast to all this.

In his celebrated address on Pushkin, Dostoyevsky calls the restless heroes of Russian literature, beginning with Pushkin's Aleko and Eugene Onegin, 'wayfarers'. They were indeed wayfarers, for the disharmony of their existence was felt more strongly when they were strangers to such surroundings, or had been plucked away from them and placed in new circumstances. With Turgenev and Tolstoy the landscape is an expression and embodiment of the traditional, natural harmony.

Dostoyevsky's settings—always very precise and even documentary—express the disharmony of life. Despite their precision, they are ghostly and fantastic. This is especially true of his descriptions of St Petersburg. There is a characteristic passage in a letter he wrote in 1861:

'I recall a wintry January evening. I was hurrying home from Vyborgsky District. I was very young. When I reached the Neva, I halted for a moment and looked intently down the river into the bleak, murky distance, lit suddenly by the last crimson rays of the sun setting behind the turbid horizon. Night was enveloping the city, and the last sunlight scattered countless myriads of sparks in the scintillating flakes of frozen snow filling the wide valley of the Neva. The temperature must have dropped to twenty degrees below zero Centigrade. Clouds of cold vapour hovered over tired horses and scurrying people. The slightest sound caused the compressed air to vibrate. Columns of smoke ascended from the rooftops on both sides of the river and soared like monsters into the cold sky, until new buildings seemed to tower over the old ones and a new city arose in the sky . . . And at last the whole world, with all its inhabitants, strong and weak, with all its dwellings, from beggar asylums to gilded mansions, loomed in the murky dusk like a fantastic, magic vision, a ghostly image that, it seemed, would also vanish and billow up into the dark-blue sky in a cloud of steam.'

To Dostoyevsky and his heroes, Petersburg was always a phantom city. We will return to this later, but at this point we may note only that to Dostoyevsky real existence is inseparable from a harmony that does not ignore individual fates. Disharmony appears to Dostoyevsky as something unreal and fantastic, an oppressive nightmare from which a person is unable to wake up.

In the spring of 1845 Dostoyevsky finished his novel *Poor Folk*, a story of hopeless, passive, meek despair. It brought him fame, and the friendship of Nekrasov and Belinsky. Then followed disillusionment, ideological differences with Belinsky's circle and a breach between the two men. Dostoyevsky joined a revolutionary circle, and in 1849 he was sentenced to death for his participation in it. The sentence was commuted to hard labour (in singularly sadistic circumstances, it must be said, for the reprieve was announced only after all the preliminaries of the execution had been carried out and the condemned were facing the firing squad). Prison was a period of reappraisal. Dostoyevsky turned against his youthful revolutionary ideals, though he could not forget or retract them altogether. He became an advocate of autocracy and orthodoxy. But Dostoyevsky's creative art possessed a logic of its own. In the 1860s he began a series of novels which to this day retain all their power to destroy the traditional forces of oppression and humiliation.

The first of this series, *Crime and Punishment*, was written in 1865, a difficult period in Dostoyevsky's life. His elder brother had died shortly before, leaving a big family on his hands. Soon after that, the magazine Dostoyevsky was publishing closed down. Dostoyevsky's circumstances became straitened in the extreme and he was reduced to a state of the utmost destitution, feverishly attempting to evade imprisonment for debt and secure postponements of payment. His life was a constant round of visits to loan offices, money-lenders, solicitors—and police stations. Added to his poverty was the backbreaking work of spending sleepless nights poring over galley-proofs, and dealing with the censors. Dostoyevsky sought escape abroad, but there too he experienced poverty, not to mention downright starvation. He even had no candles to write by in his cold hotel room. It was in such circumstances that *Crime and Punishment* was written.

Raskolnikov, the main hero of the novel, exhausted by poverty (here the narrative is practically autobiographical), ill and embittered, nurses the idea of the permissibility of a crime if it leads to great and possibly useful results. A man has a right, even an obligation, to commit murder if the victim is a worthless creature and if the act opens up the way to great undertakings. The fate of a speck of dust, an atom, a micro-organism, is immaterial to the destiny of the world, and a micro-organism must be crushed if it is in the way of a 'macroscopic' subject. The old woman money-lender whom Raskolnikov murders is just such a creature.

As in most of his novels, Dostoyevsky introduces a supplementary character to set off the main hero more vividly. This is Svidrigaylov, a man who holds the view that 'everything is permissible' and ends up in spiritual bankruptcy and suicide. The contrast between the two men is a kind of limiting transition which indicates to what depths, in Dostoyevsky's view, a mind that rebels against traditional beliefs can fall. Traditional beliefs are voiced by the positive characters. Among these is Sonia Marmeladova, driven by poverty into the streets of Petersburg, who listens to Raskolnikov's confession when he can no longer bear the weight of his crime.

Crime and Punishment is the pinnacle of Dostoyevsky's creative work. Nowhere else does he use the establishment of atmosphere, the succession of characters, and indeed the total structure of the book, to reveal with such precision the *actual* message of its characters.

The word 'actual' has been italicised to stress the fact that the actual message is generally opposed to Dostoyevsky's own ideas, to his subjective views and intentions. It is the artistic potential of *Crime and Punishment*, what has been called its poetics, that is responsible for the message actually conveyed through the characters. There is a subtle inter-relationship between the poetics of the book and its characters. It is reciprocal, in that poetics is not a *linear* function of the author's intention or of the characters he has conjured into life. Just as the instruments a scientist uses to observe physical processes affect those processes to a greater or lesser degree, so the means of creative representation of reality tend to shift the angle of view and give the reader an insight into things that are not part of the author's subjective intention.

The poetics of *Crime and Punishment* is rational in nature. The characters of the book speak like people possessed by thoughts—paradoxical thoughts, maybe, bogged down in contradictions and feverish, but nevertheless thoughts. Passion serves as an accompaniment to thoughts, usually in the shape of a desire to assert, verify and test them. The heroes' moods are rarely unaccountable; even when they appear to be so, they are soon explained and turn out to be collisions of thought. The setting in Petersburg—like the settings of Dostoyevsky's other novels—affects the hero's thoughts. The gloomy, oppressive atmosphere in which the opening episodes of *Crime and Punishment* unfold arouses an unaccountable depression in the hero. But within a page we find that his mood is in actual fact due to agonising reflection on the infinite complexity of life. Raskolnikov's characteristic manner of speaking, stumbling and incoherent, is wholly determined by his train of thought, which is also stumbling, incoherent and contradictory.

The overall impression that the reader forms from the rationalist poetics of *Crime and Punishment* can be formulated as follows: thought capable of bold and paradoxical modification cannot lead one into a moral blind alley; on the contrary, it is capable of resolving all contradictions. This conclusion is in sharp contrast to the events on the surface of the novel, where reason without faith leads to moral catastrophe.

Dostoyevsky's next philosophical novel, *The Idiot*, came out in 1868. To judge from early drafts, he regarded Prince Myshkin, the chief character, as a supreme hero-figure comparable with Don Quixote or, indeed, with Christ.

Nastasya Filippovna is one of the most complex women in world literature. Her emotions are deep, and her thoughts even more so. Her sudden changes of mood and her paradoxical actions are manifestations of a state of thought, not a state of mind. In the end she comes to the conclusion that she is unworthy of Prince Myshkin, who loves her and whom she loves. The reader responds to the musicality of the character, he perceives the intellectual element in her anguish, he accepts as logical, though paradoxical, her sudden flight from the altar and her descent into the depths of irrationality, symbolised by the character of the merchant Rogozhin, who kills her. Myshkin too, sinks into the same irrational depths. His madness returns and this time finally.

Dostoyevsky may have conceived this calvary of meekness and forgivingness, like the calvary of Christ, as a symbol of the moral triumph of crucified souls. None the less, the poetics of *The Idiot* suggests that here we have a tragedy of thought that is incapable of overcoming tradition and traditional concepts, thought that is not paradoxical enough, not 'non-Euclidean' enough.

The reader is much too charmed by the heroes' intellectual life to regard them as martyrs or apostles of anti-intellectual tradition.

Whatever Dostoyevsky's anti-rationalist intentions, his rationalist poetics points to conclusions that belie them. His poetics are revealed in the musicality of the book and the naturalness of the dialogues, scenes and events. This is an intellectual musicality. Even Nastasya Filippovna's appearance reflects her intellectual charm. At the beginning of the novel Myshkin sees a portrait of her, hanging on the wall. Dostoyevsky describes it in considerable detail, and one is reminded of the 'Mona Lisa', that rationalist ideal of Renaissance portrait painting. When men argue about the enigmatic smile of the Florentine they are concerned not so much with emotions as with *thoughts*, partially hidden, that express the basic character of the age. No heroine of Russian literature can compare with Nastasya Filippovna in emotional or intellectual intensity, in the acuteness of her intellectual conflicts or her own dependence on those conflicts.

As time passed, Dostoyevsky's reactionary tendencies came to dominate him, and he filled his books with lengthy invectives against the claims of reason. In 1871–2 he wrote *The Possessed*, a pamphlet novel directed against democratic revolutionary circles. The central character, Nikolai Stavrogin, is a man with no moral standards whatsoever, who sees not the slightest difference between a great exploit and a great crime.

' "Is it true," ' asks Shatov, another of the novel's principal characters, ' "that you declared that you saw no aesthetic distinction between some brutally obscene action and a great exploit, such as the sacrifice of one's life for the good of humanity? Is it true that you have found identical beauty, equal enjoyment in both extremes?"

' "It's impossible to answer a question of that kind—I won't answer," muttered Stavrogin, who might well have got up and gone away, but who did not get up and go away.

' "I don't know, either, why evil is hateful and good is beautiful, but I do know why the sense of that distinction is effaced and lost in people like the Stavrogins," Shatov persisted, trembling all over. "Do you know why you made that base and shameful marriage of yours? Simply because the shame and senselessness of it reached the pitch of genius! You are not one of those who hesitate on the brink! You dive in, head foremost. You married out of a passion for martyrdom, out of a craving for remorse, and through sheer moral sensuality. It was a laceration of the nerves . . . The defiance of common sense was too tempting." '[1]

Stavrogin is attracted not so much by moral sensuality as by experimental sensuality. In effect, every scene involving him is an experiment in which his only concern is to measure the heights or depths of which his partner is capable.

[1] Dostoyevsky, *The Possessed*, translated by Constance Garnett (J. M. Dent & Sons, 1960), vol. 1, p. 233–4.

Dostoyevsky is striving to show that thought alone, without traditional faith, cannot serve as a basis for morality, that rationalism is itself immoral, and provides inadequate answers to moral questions. He provides Stavrogin with a shadow, Pyotr Verkhovensky, whose relationship to him is the same as that of Svidrigaylov to Raskolnikov: he exposes the moral abyss into which, in Dostoyevsky's view, the rebellion of reason against traditional faith leads. Another figure whom Dostoyevsky introduces is Stepan Verkhovensky, an old liberal idealist of the 1840s. Dostoyevsky's purpose here is to include in one group the whole of the liberal and radical intelligentsia, from the ludicrous and apparently harmless Stepan Verkhovensky, whom the new generation rejects, to the horrifying Pyotr Verkhovensky. The central figure who embodies immoral rationalism is Stavrogin.

This is the intention of *The Possessed*. Its poetics, however, demolishes the author's intention. Driven by his recollections of the past, Dostoyevsky imposes on the character of Stepan Verkhovensky something of the great thinkers of the 1840s, until finally he is forced to concede that Stepan is akin to the character of Granovsky, 'that purest of men'. The poetics also demolishes his intentions for Pyotr Verkhovensky; as the character acquires substance and reality, the logic of the poetics makes it impossible to treat him as a collective image of the radical intelligentsia. In fact, he is clearly opposed to that intelligentsia. Dostoyevsky loses control over Stavrogin, as well: he cannot make Stavrogin a participant in the revolutionary movement, his very creative instinct cries out against this. The upshot is that what was intended as a pamphlet directed against the revolutionary intelligentsia turns out to be a question addressed to the future: in what circumstances can reason lead to *one-value morality*, to the safeguarding and preservation of every human life?

That reason, not tradition, must produce this morality is seen in the rationalist fabric of the novel, where every moral criterion is the outcome of mental effort, often extremely painful, which, however, never accepts tradition as the source of moral solutions.

In 1875, four years after *The Possessed*, in his novel *The Raw Youth*, Dostoyevsky came very close to analysing out the causes of immorality and in particular its social origins. The book presents a gallery of realistically portrayed exponents of the creed of gain and violence. They are not radical intellectuals by a long chalk, and their actions are not guided by unfettered thought. Most significant, however, *The Raw Youth* presents a vivid portrayal of the collapse of the traditional mainstays of Russian life, the disintegration of the family and the rise of individualistic tendencies. The novel abounds in details that clearly reveal the historic roots of this disintegration.

The conflict between intention and performance reached its climax with Dostoyevsky's work in 1879–80. He thought that his new novel, *The Brothers Karamazov*, would present the decisive engagement in the struggle between traditional faith and rebellious reason, in which the latter would be disgraced. He set the stage accordingly. Reason is represented by Ivan Karamazov, who argues tellingly against the providential harmony of reality. Dostoyevsky attaches several 'interpreters' to him, whose task it is to prepare his defeat. The chief of these is Smerdyakov, valet of the brothers' father. He draws from Ivan's advocacy of the sovereignty of reason the practical conclusion that, if 'everything is permissible', he is free to murder his master. The second of these interpreters is the devil, who appears to Ivan Karamazov as an embodiment of his innermost thoughts. The third is the 'Great Inquisitor' from Ivan's poem, who contrasts the Catholic ideal of universal despotism with the gentle teachings of Christ.

Traditional faith is represented by the youngest of the Karamazov brothers, Alyosha, whom Dostoyevsky provides with a powerful ally in the person of his teacher, Father Zossima.

The struggle that was to have been enacted between the covers of *The Brothers Karamazov* aroused both the hopes and apprehensions of reactionary circles, and notably of the Russian government. At that time Dostoyevsky frequently met and corresponded with Konstantin Pobedonostsev, the prime minister, a fanatical conservative. He assured him that Ivan Karamazov's apparently irresistible attacks on the harmony of reality would be refuted by the death-bed precepts of Father Zossima. The philosophy of Russian nihilism, Dostoyevsky declared, would be repudiated.

But Ivan Karamazov's arguments are set forth with such a convincing renunciation of the personal and with such authenticity that they have become immortal. The attack on 'providential harmony' proved even more prophetic. It has retained its vigour and interest to this day.

Dostoyevsky wrote to Pobedonostsev that he had allowed Ivan Karamazov to speak so compellingly from an overwhelming sense of realism. But what was 'realism' to Dostoyevsky? We shall consider the question in detail later on, but we may note here a basic feature of Dostoyevsky's realism: it was *experimental*. Dostoyevsky verified his initial conceptions by placing his heroes in extremely testing circumstance. His results are paradoxical, breaking completely with tradition and sometimes running quite contrary to his own expectations. Pushkin once complained in a letter that Tatyana Larina's marriage in *Eugene Onegin* had come as a complete surprise to him. This is characteristic of artistic creation and, for that matter, of any creative activity. Through Dostoyevsky's experimental method, the evolution of his characters reveals things that are latent, unperceived, or suppressed by *a priori* tendencies in his mind. As against subjective intentions, the objective logic of his creative powers leads to a situation in which the artist is not so much concerned with constructing and inventing characters, actions and dialogue as with *discovering* them. It was simply impossible for Dostoyevsky to keep Ivan Karamazov silent, because his conversation with Alyosha and his dialogue with the devil are experiments whose outcome concerned Dostoyevsky more intimately and tragically than the fulfilment of his promises to Pobedonostsev (and to himself!), made at a time when he was still considering the social impact of the book. He *never* really recognised the traditional faith: though as a pamphleteer he defended it against the encroachments of reason, he demolished it in his role as a great artist. Shatov's reply to Stavrogin is characteristic:

' "But you want a hare?" ' Shatov asks.

' "Wh–a–t?"

' "Your own nasty expression." Shatov laughed spitefully, sitting down again. "To cook your hare you must first catch it; to believe in God you must first have a god. You used to say that in Petersburg, I'm told, like Nozdryov, who tried to catch a hare by its hind legs."

' "No, what he did was to boast he'd caught it. Now let me ask you a question. I think I have the right to ask one now. Tell me, have you caught your hare?"

' "Don't dare to ask me in that way. Ask me differently, quite differently." Shatov suddenly began trembling all over.

' "Certainly I'll ask differently." Nikolai Vsevolodovich looked coldly at him. "I only wanted to know, do you believe in God yourself?"

23

' "I believe in Russia. . . . I believe in her orthodoxy. . . . I believe in the body of Christ. . . . I believe that the new advent will take place in Russia. . . . I believe . . ." Shatov muttered frantically.

' "And in God? In God?"

' "I . . . I will believe in God." '[1]

Dostoyevsky the pamphleteer hoped to come to terms with a simple 'Euclidean' faith. Dostoyevsky the artist refused to come to terms with anything; he wanted to *know*, and this desire acquired a dimension corresponding to his genius. It coloured his poetics and was itself nurtured by poetry. It was a craving for harmony. Here indeed lie the points of contact between Dostoyevsky's artistic creativity and Einstein's scientific creativity.

[1] Dostoyevsky, *The Possessed*, op. cit., p. 232.

2

The Non-Euclidean World

Dostoyevsky's creative work is a nineteenth-century question posed to the twentieth century. But why should it be addressed to science, and specifically to theoretical physics? How can we say that Einstein's ideas have in some respects answered it?

The conception of a world harmony that does not ignore the fate of the individual is fully relevant to science. Already in the nineteenth century the social and moral ideals of society were, unlike the Utopias of the past, associated with objective, casual, essentially scientific analyses of social processes. Social science developed theories linking social progress with the expansion of production. By the end of the century, so-called 'abstract' scientific ideas began to demonstrate their value for the practical advancement of mankind. Dostoyevsky, who was out of sympathy with the progressive social ideas of his time and openly opposed them, none the less expressed them unconsciously in his creative writing. Unlike Dostoyevsky the thinker, who upheld traditional dogmas, Dostoyevsky the artist proceeded objectively and experimentally, by a series of psychological observations, which under his pen turned into social observations, or even by straight social reporting.

But to illustrate the historical value of juxtaposing Dostoyevsky and Einstein we must examine the features of twentieth-century science that connect it with moral problems, with the search for moral harmony.

The turn of the century was a time when science acutely felt the need for a systematic explanation of paradoxical experimental findings. In contrast with *ad hoc* scientific theories, invented specifically to explain certain observations, Einstein used the word 'systematic' to distinguish theories capable of deducing the results of experiments from the most general physical postulates embracing the whole of the universe. Such a systematic deduction of paradoxical experimental results from paradoxical general postulates is characteristic of Einstein's method. Rejection of a traditional initial premise can cause an observation that had seemed paradoxical, inexplicable or 'miraculous' to appear a natural deduction from theory. Scientific analysis is a flight from wonder, and in selecting a scientific theory one should be guided by the criteria of 'external confirmation' and 'inner perfection'. Einstein defines the former criterion as agreement of theory and observation, and the latter as the 'naturalness' of a theory, its derivation from the most general postulates, with a minimum of *ad hoc* explanations of observed facts. The two criteria are connected by the principle of *physical meaningfulness*: that is, the initial postulates must, as a matter of principle, allow for verification by observation and experiment.

In so far as the world is governed by knowable laws, its structure is objective and orderly; the world is not a chaos, it is a harmonious whole in which man discovers unified causal laws, and in which relationships agreeing with observations can be deduced from initial general principles. The implications of this are important for an understanding of Einstein's work. In his autobiography, written in 1949, Einstein wrote of his longing to understand the 'extra-personal' which had inspired him since adolescence.

'Out yonder there was this huge world, which exists independently of us human beings and which stands before us like a vast, eternal riddle, at least partially accessible to observation and analysis. To study such a world sets free one's mind. I soon noticed that many a man whom I had learned to respect had found inner freedom and security in this discipline. Intellectual understanding of the extra-personal world, so far as it was attainable, presented itself as a goal, half realised and half unrealised before my mind's eye. Men from the present day and from the past who had accepted the same goal, would be my companions on the journey, and so too would be the discoveries they had made. The road to this paradise was not as easy and attractive as the road to the religious paradise; but it has proved itself as trustworthy, and I have never regretted having chosen it.'[1]

To Einstein the harmony of the universe was inseparable from moral ideals. In his way of thinking he was close to Feuerbach, who found a counterpoint between the other theological levels—between ideals and nature. ('Moral eminence is the ideal which every man must set himself if he hopes to achieve anything; but this ideal is—and should be—a human ideal and purpose. The natural eminence above man is nature itself.[2])

Einstein's reverence for nature stemmed from his moral ideal, the rejection of selfish desires.

'The scientist', he wrote 'is possessed by the sense of

[1] Albert Einstein, *Autobiographical Notes*, printed in *Albert Einstein: Philosopher-Scientist*, Ed. Paul A. Schilp (Tudor, New York, 1951), p. 5.
[2] Einstein *Comment je vois le monde* (Paris, 1934), p. 39.

27

universal causation. The future, to him, is every whit as necessary and determined as the past. There is nothing divine about morality; it is a purely human affair. His religious feeling takes the form of a rapturous amazement at the harmony of natural law. . . . This feeling is the guiding principle of his life and work, in so far as he succeeds in keeping himself from the shackles of selfish desire.'[1]

This 'guiding principle of . . . life and work' is common to Einstein and the great rationalists of the seventeenth century, Spinoza pre-eminently. Spinoza's moral ideals and his attitude towards nature are linked by what Pascal called 'renunciation of the hated "self" '. This tendency is linked with the desire for objective knowledge and the exclusion of all subjective, anthropomorphic and anthropocentric concepts. It was in this context that the idea of relativity originated and evolved. The most important result of this line of thinking in the seventeenth century was the heliocentric system; in the twentieth century it was Einstein's theory of relativity.

In order to gain a clearer view of the relationship between the relativity theory and Einstein's general ideas, and its relevance to what we have called 'the answer of the twentieth century to the questions of the nineteenth', we must take a closer look at the content of the relativity theory.

Towards the end of the nineteenth century it was established that light propagates with the same velocity in all systems moving relative to one another and without acceleration, i.e. uniformly and in a straight line. This paradoxical experimental result contradicted the classical rule of the composition of velocities. On this hypothesis, light could be compared to a passenger in a train, walking along the corridor, whose speed in relation to the track is always the

[1] Einstein, *Ideas and Opinions* (Alvin Redman, London, 1956), p. 40.

28

same, regardless of whether the train is moving or not, or of whether he is walking towards the locomotive or away from it—that is, regardless also of whether the speed with which he is walking must be added to or subtracted from the velocity of the train. If light travels with the same velocity both in a given system and in another system moving without acceleration, relative to the first, then it must be impossible to detect the original system's movement by any optical experiments. It must, in fact, be impossible to detect uniform motion in a straight line by observing physical processes within a given system. The concept of motion only has meaning in so far as a moving system changes its position in relation to other bodies. In short, motion has only a relative meaning.

Physical processes, Einstein says, are independent of a system's uniform rectilinear motion. 'Imagine two physicists', he says. 'Each one has a laboratory at his disposal, equipped with every conceivable physical instrument. Suppose that one laboratory is situated in an open field, and the other is in a railway carriage travelling with uniform speed in a certain direction. The principle of relativity states that if the two physicists use their instruments to study the laws of nature they will both discover the same laws, provided that the train is moving uniformly and without jolts. In more general terms we can say: according to the principle of relativity, the laws of nature do not depend on the translational motion of reference systems.'[1]

The theory of relativity is an example of a systematic explanation of experimental results based on the general structure of the universe and on generalised hypotheses. In a letter to Maurice Solovine, Einstein writes:

'In spite of the diversity of the physical experiments which

[1] Einstein, *Comment je vois le monde* (Paris, 1934), p. 143.

constitute the basis of the relativity theory, its method and content can be summed up in a few words. Contrary to the fact, known already to the ancients, that motion can be perceived only *relatively*, physics based itself on the concept of *absolute* motion. In optics it was assumed that there existed a kind of motion different from all others, namely, motion through the luminiferous ether, to which the motion of all corporeal bodies could be referred. The luminiferous ether thus represented an embodiment of the concept of absolute rest. If the stationary luminiferous ether pervading the whole of space really existed, motion could be referred to it, thereby acquiring absolute meaning. This concept could serve as the basis of mechanics. However, with the failure of all attempts to detect motion of this kind, the problem had to be reconsidered. This was tackled systematically in the relativity theory. It assumes the absence of privileged states of motion in nature and analyses the conclusions deriving from this assumption. Its method is analogous to the method of thermodynamics. The latter represents no more than a systematised answer to the question: What are the laws of nature that make the construction of a *perpetuum mobile* impossible?'[1]

One of the fundamental concepts that dispose of absolute motion is the velocity of light as the limiting velocity of physical entities. If a particle that existed at one point occurs at another point sooner than the distance between the two points can be covered by light, the newly arrived particle cannot be identified with the earlier one. An immutable, self-identical physical object cannot travel at a velocity greater than that of light. Renewed impulses applied to a particle cannot make its velocity increase indefinitely. As the velocity approaches the speed of light, new impulses will

[1] Einstein, *Lettres à Maurice Solovine* (Paris, 1956), p. 19.

cause smaller and smaller accelerations. In other words, the particle's mass increases with its velocity. Its energy of motion and its mass are related in direct proportion. Energy equals mass times the square of the velocity of light. Einstein assumed that the mass of a body at rest was proportional to its inner energy. Nuclear energy techniques, which make use of the fact that the change in the internal energy of atomic nuclei is proportional to the change of their mass, are a confirmation of Einstein's theory. Einstein was thus the prophet of the nuclear era.

The physical relevance of the basic premises of relativity theory became apparent after it had been embodied in the formalism of four-dimensional geometry, in which a point is characterised by three spatial co-ordinates and a fourth, temporal co-ordinate.

Newton's mechanics allowed for the propagation of physical processes at infinite velocity through space. If an interaction between bodies propagates instantaneously, i.e. if one and the same action emanates from one body and reaches the other at the same instant we have a purely spatial process, a process occupying zero time. In that case, three-dimensional space possesses a real, physical equivalent, which allows of experimental verification. Instants occurring simultaneously over all space add up to absolute time. It is, in an absolute sense, a flux of simultaneous instants embracing the whole of the universe.

In Einstein's mechanics there are no physical equivalents of three-dimensional geometry. There is no instantaneous action at a distance. Einstein's mechanics does not allow for the synchronisation of events which are defined in different frames of reference. If a stationary ether existed, events could be synchronised by sending out signals to an equal distance in different directions: they would arrive at the distant points at the same time, simultaneously in the absolute sense. In the absence of the ether as an absolute frame of reference, however, the signals will arrive simultaneously at two different equidistant points only if they are moving together with the signal source, if they belong to the same frame of reference. In any other system the points will be moving in relation to the signal source, and the signals may arrive at different instants. Events that are simultaneous in one frame of reference turn out to be non-simultaneous in another. In general it is impossible to synchronise remote events. The concept of absolute time is physically meaningless. Hence, space with no temporal dimension, 'instantaneous' space, is a purely geometric, not a physical concept. Only four-dimensional diversity, in which every point is characterised by four co-ordinates, three spatial and one temporal, possesses physical reality. Such a point is known as a world point. At any given point at a given moment, an event, e.g. a particle, may occur. A succession of events— the particle's motion—is described by its world line. Ultimately, all events in the universe are composed of such motions. Can we say that the real world consists of world lines? We shall see that this question is linked with the most fundamental problems of the universe. We shall also find analogies that connect it with problems that are far removed from physics.

So far we have been speaking of the *special* theory of relativity, which Einstein enunciated in 1905. It postulates the relativity of rectilinear uniform motion and the equality of all reference systems moving relative to one another without acceleration. In 1912–16 Einstein generalised the principle of relativity to include accelerated motion. Motion with acceleration, like uniform motion, cannot be detected from the course of physical processes in a moving system.

When two systems are moving with acceleration relative to one another, both are equally valid, and physical processes take place uniformly in them. Accelerated motion, like inertial, coasting motion, is a physically meaningful concept only when one speaks of relative motion, of the change in distance between two bodies, one of which is taken as a reference body. Owing to their equality, either system can be regarded as being motionless and the other as moving, without affecting the nature of their internal processes.

All scientists from Newton until the time of Einstein have been satisfied that there exist absolute criteria of accelerated motion. According to this view, the transformation just mentioned (in which a moving system is treated as stationary, and a stationary system as moving) changes the course of the internal processes in the systems. We have all observed inertial forces at work in an accelerated system: the jolt that throws a person forward when a train brakes rapidly, and the force that presses him back into his seat when it begins to accelerate. Newton, for obvious reasons, did not use such examples, but he devised one for himself; in a rotating bucket centrifugal forces cause water to rise up the sides, which would not happen if the bucket were fixed and the world revolving about it. In the light of this discrepancy, how can accelerated motions be brought under the relativity principle?

Einstein made use of the following argument. The inertial forces generated by the accelerated motion of a system are in principle indistinguishable from gravitational forces. If a system is moving upwards with an acceleration equal to the acceleration of gravity, bodies within the system will experience a downward pull, which we would ascribe to the inertial forces. Equally, in a stationary system acted upon by gravity, the gravitational forces will affect all bodies within the system, and the downward pull will be the same as in the system moving upwards with acceleration. It would be another matter if an electrical field were acting instead of a gravitational field, because this acts on bodies differently according to their electrical charges. But gravity acts in proportion to the inertial mass, and therefore gravitational forces are indistinguishable from inertial forces due to acceleration. Hence, the inertial forces that distinguish an 'absolutely unaccelerated' body can be treated as gravitational forces without altering the processes observed in the system.

The fundamental property of gravity, the uniformity of its action on all bodies, makes it possible to regard gravity as a *warping of space-time*. In arguing this, Einstein assumed that light possesses mass and that a beam of light is attracted and deflected by a heavy body. (In 1919 this assumption was confirmed by astronomical observation.) Now all physical prototypes of a straight line—that is, the motions of physical objects in a straight line—are found to be dependent on gravitational fields. In relativity theory, a physical prototype follows a four-dimensional, spatio-temporal world line. (A purely spatial line has no physical meaning, no physical existence.) What, then, is a straight world line? If a body is moving non-uniformly—that is to say, with acceleration— along a straight spatial line, its *world* line is curved, just as it is curved in the case of uniform motion in a curved spatial path. Any violation of uniform rectilinear motion can be treated as a curving of a four-dimensional, spatio-temporal world line. If some force causes the uniform acceleration of all bodies and of light (which is how a gravitational field acts), then one can speak of space-time curvature.

It is simple to imagine a curved line or surface. It is very difficult to imagine the curving of three-dimensional space or four-dimensional space-time. However, if one draws geometrical figures on a curved surface (a sphere, for example), they will possess different properties from those found in *Euclidean* geometry. In a triangle on such a surface the sum of the angles is greater than two right angles. Since figures made up of four-dimensional world lines prove to obey this kind of *non-Euclidean* geometry we can speak of space-time curvature. In such a way the general theory of relativity is able to treat gravitational fields as a curving of space-time. So much for gravity. But does four-dimensional, non-Euclidean geometry apply to all natural processes without exception? The first of these to be discovered and studied was electromagnetic fields. Can the geometry of the world be generalised in such a manner as to explain the existence of fields other than gravitational? This was the problem which worried Einstein for more than thirty years, from the 1920s till his death in 1955. In the next chapter we shall dwell on his search for a unified field theory. We shall also discuss the emotional equivalents of the search for cosmic harmony that constituted the leitmotif of Einstein's discoveries in physics. It was these equivalents that added a subtle, psychological overtone to his search for a unified field theory. To some extent they explain the connection between Einstein's moral and aesthetic principles and his scientific achievements.

3
The Craving for Harmony

An appropriate illustration to the general moral and psychological problems of today is the tragedy of Hamlet, represented by Shakespeare in such depth that, centuries later, conflicts of this kind appear as recapitulations of Shakespeare's drama. Hamlet seeks to transform thought into action, and to him avenging his father means restoring world harmony. The idea of world harmony is a fundamental idea of the new times.

Spinoza linked moral harmony with cosmic harmony, with the search for unified laws governing the macrocosm and the microcosm. Rationalism extricates ethical standards from the clutches of traditional faith and links them with universal harmony. This is as true of seventeenth-century rationalism as of Einstein's rationalist world outlook. The search for cosmic harmony was a confirmation of the moral harmony, the achievements of *science* were successes of rationalist *ethics*, the defeats and setbacks of science were failures of the moral ideal. In an essay on Newton written in 1942, at the height of Nazi aggression, Einstein says that the ideas of classical mechanics are a triumph of reason, the memory of which should help man to overcome the adversities besetting him and to fight against jingoism and the cult of irrational instincts.

'Reason, of course, is weak, when measured against its never-ending tasks. Weak indeed, compared with the follies and passions of mankind, which, we must admit, almost entirely control our human destinies, in great and small things. Yet the works of understanding outlast the noisy bustling of the generations and spread light and warmth across the centuries.'[1]

Einstein speaks of the classical ideal: a scheme according to which the universe consists of nothing but bodies moving relative to one another. The theory of relativity rid the classical ideal of the alien references to absolute time and absolute space. Relativity is a step towards the classical ideal, which Einstein called 'Newton's programme'; its contribution to this 'programme' is the removal of blemishes from Newtonian mechanics. As Einstein wrote of Newton:

'Such a man can be understood only by thinking of him as a stage on which the struggle for eternal truth took place. Long before Newton there had been vigorous minds who conceived that it ought to be possible, by purely logical deduction from simple physical hypotheses, to give cogent explanations of the phenomena that were perceptible to the senses. But Newton was the first to succeed in finding a clearly formulated basis from which he could deduce a wide field of phenomena by means of mathematical thinking, logically, quantitatively and in harmony with experience.'[2]

The programme designed to remove the blemishes from the classical ideal was never completed. First, absolute space was eliminated from the world picture for uniform motion in a straight line. Then, in the general theory of relativity, it was eliminated from accelerated motion with the help of the

[1] Einstein, *Out of My Later Years* (Thames and Hudson, London, 1950), p. 220.
[2] Ibid., p. 219.

37

concept of space-time curvature, with which gravitational fields were identified. Subsequent attempts to identify other fields with changes in the geometric properties of space-time proved unsuccessful. Einstein advanced some highly ingenious ideas; he generalised geometrical relationships in an attempt to find other properties of space-time besides curvature which could be identified with the electromagnetic field. From non-Euclidean geometry, with its rejection of Euclid's parallel lines postulate, he passed on to even more paradoxical geometries. They possessed a degree of 'inner perfection', in that physical laws were derived from very general premises. It was a different matter, however, when it came to 'external confirmation'. Einstein's outlines of the unified field theory did not actually contradict the facts. They simply defied experimental verification. They did not yield conclusions for which an experiment could state, uniquely: 'Yes, this concept alone explains the result. Other ideas contradict our observations.' Einstein could not conceive the *experimentum crucis*, the crucial test of his theory, with the result that the various versions of the unified field theory lacked physical meaningfulness.

In 1944 Einstein wrote to his old friend, Hans Muhsam: 'I may still live to see whether I am justified in believing in my equations. It is no more than a hope, as every variant entails tremendous mathematical difficulties. I have not written to you for so long, in spite of a troubled conscience and the claims of friendship, because I am in an agony of mathematical torment from which I am unable to escape.'[1]

Somewhat earlier Einstein had written to Muhsam: 'I am an old man, known mainly as a crank who doesn't like to wear socks. But I am working at a more fantastic rate than ever,

[1] Helle Zeit—Dunkle Zeit, *In Memoriam Albert Einstein*, edited by Carl Seelig (Europa Verlag, Zürich, 1956), S. 51.

and I still hope to solve my pet problem of the unified physical field. I feel as though I were flying in an airplane high up in the sky, without quite knowing how I will ever reach the ground . . . I hope to live to see better times and catch a glimpse of a promised land of sorts.'[1]

To Einstein the unified field theory was an expression of the logical harmony of the universe. As he once remarked to his assistant, Ernst Strauss, 'What interests me is: could God have made the world differently? Does the requirement of logical simplicity leave any latitude?'

Einstein dwells on this question in his *Autobiographical Notes*. Science, he says, deals with apparently primary, empirical physical constants that are not logically derivable from other quantities. They could have other numerical values without in the least affecting the scheme of the universe. The distances between galaxies and between stars, the mean radii of planetary orbits, the radii of planets themselves and even the radii of particles, are different. But maybe these constants are uniquely determined by the universal scheme, and 'God' could not have 'made the world differently' ('God' being an ironical pseudonym for world harmony)? Does world harmony—the requirement of logical simplicity—determine physical constants *uniquely*?

'Concerning such constants', Einstein writes, 'I would like to state a theorem which at present cannot be based upon anything more than an act of faith; there are no *arbitrary* constants—that is to say, nature is so constituted that it is logically possible to establish such rigorous laws that they demand uniquely determined constants, whose numerical value could not be changed without destroying the theory.'[2]

If the requirement of logical simplicity leaves no latitude,

[1] Ibid., S. 50–1.
[2] Einstein, *Autobiographical Notes*, op. cit., p. 63.

if the unified logical scheme of reality allows for no process, *however* microscopic, to be independent of or indifferent to it, then any individual microscopic process which contradicts world harmony destroys it or leaves it unrealised. There can be no such thing as a rational whole based on irrational microscopic elements.

The development of the calculus of infinitesimals, in the seventeenth century, gave rise to two widely differing concepts of physical prototypes. For Leibniz, an infinitesimal was like a grain of sand to a planet; its fate was of no consequence whatsoever to the fate of the planet. An infinitesimal was a finite but negligible quantity.

The other concept treated infinitesimals as quantities that could be made infinitely smaller, the limiting relationships existing between them bearing testimony to the limitless precision to which the rational laws of the universe were valid.

Einstein accepted this second concept as a basic physical idea. He was dissatisfied with the statistical concept of the microcosm, according to which the general laws of nature state the *probability* of microscopic processes, and approach certainty only for very large populations. On this view, individual microscopic processes may well fail to obey the macroscopic laws. This, essentially, is the concept on which quantum mechanics, developed in 1924–5, is based. We shall discuss this in the next chapter. Here we shall only note that Einstein's continuous 'grumbling', to use Max Planck's words, about quantum mechanics was mainly due to intuitive prejudice. Einstein's specific arguments were successfully refuted by Niels Bohr, but this did not convince Einstein. He conceded that quantum mechanics agreed with all the facts, did not lead to contradictions, and even interpreted some of the facts. But, he pointed out, one should not make a virtue of necessity. Quantum mechanics contradicted his scientific intuition. In 1947 he wrote to Max Born:

'In our scientific expectations we have moved towards opposed points of view. You believe in a dice-playing god, and I in the perfect rule of law in a world of objective reality. I have tried to define this in a wildly speculative way and I hope that somebody else will find a more tangible basis for the concept than is given to me.'[1]

In another letter Einstein stressed the purely intuitive character of his certainty of the non-statistical nature of the basic laws of reality.

'I cannot substantiate my attitude to physics in a way that you would find rational. I see, of course, that the statistical interpretation (the necessity of which, in the frame of the existing formalism, was first clearly recognised by yourself) has a considerable content of truth. Yet I cannot seriously believe it, because the theory is inconsistent with the principle that physics has to represent a reality in space and time, without the ghost of action at a distance . . . I am absolutely convinced that we shall eventually arrive at a theory in which the objects connected by laws are not probabilities, but facts, such as one took for granted only a short time ago. However, I cannot provide logical arguments for my conviction. I can only call on my little finger as a witness, which claims no authority outside my own skin.'[2]

'God does not play dice.' Einstein's 'God' must always be thought of in ironical inverted commas. It is nothing like Dostoyevsky's God, for Dostoyevsky, even if, like Shatov, he did question the existence of God ('. . . I will believe in

[1] Max Born, *Natural Philosophy of Cause and Chance* (Clarendon Press, Oxford, 1949), p. 122.
[2] Ibid.

God'), forced himself to believe and sought relief in faith. Our concern, however, is not Dostoyevsky the thinker, nor the characters whom he uses as the mouthpieces of his apology for orthodoxy. Our interest is Dostoyevsky the artist, and the characters who voice his doubts and queries, and his craving for moral harmony. This is Ivan Karamazov's 'God', the 'God' whose providential harmony he rejects with such logical, vivid, creative conviction. Later on, we shall return to 'Rebellion', the culminating chapter of *The Brothers Karamazov*, and see that Ivan Karamazov was dissatisfied with the statistical nature of the harmony which ignored individual fates. The 'God' who had established a providential harmony was unacceptable to him just because this harmony was based on the ignoring of microscopic irrationalities.

What is it in the 'dice-playing God', the 'God' of averages, the 'God' of statistical laws, that distresses Einstein? In a letter to James Franck, Einstein wrote:

'I can imagine that God created a world without any laws: a chaos, in short. But the notion that statistical laws are final, and that God draws lots, is highly unsympathetic to me.'[1]

Physical arguments against quantum mechanics, of course, have nothing in common with moral arguments against providential harmony. Physical arguments must be judged by their physical convincingness. Here, however, we are concerned with Einstein's moral ideals and their bearing on his search for a cosmic harmony.

In Einstein's case it was flight from the irrationalities and moral failures of everyday life that bred an interest in science. In an address on the occasion of Max Planck's sixtieth

[1] C. Seelig, *Albert Einstein. Leben und Werk Eines Genies Unsere Zeit* (Zürich, 1960), S. 396.

birthday, in 1918, Einstein spoke of the inner psychological motives that lead men to the 'temple of science'. Though he was speaking of Planck, the sentiments he expressed were autobiographical. Many people, Einstein says, take to science out of a sense of their superior intellectual power. Others are drawn to it for purely utilitarian reasons. Planck, however, belonged to another type who 'long to escape from personal life into the world of objective perception and thought. This desire', Einstein goes on, 'may be compared with the townsman's irresistible longing to escape from his noisy, cramped surroundings into the silence of high mountains, where the eye ranges freely through the still, pure air and fondly traces out the restful contours apparently built for eternity.'[1]

Most important to Einstein are the moral qualities of a scientist, his craving for the moral and social harmony which ultimately determines the range of his scientific achievement. As he wrote in an obituary to Marie Curie:

'It is the moral qualities of its leading personalities that are perhaps of even greater significance for a generation and for the course of history than their purely intellectual accomplishments. Even these latter are, to a far greater degree than is commonly credited, dependent on the stature of the character.

'I came increasingly to admire Marie Curie's human grandeur. Her strength, her purity of will, her austerity, her objectivity, her incorruptible judgements—all these were of a kind seldom found in a single individual. She felt herself at every moment to be a servant of society, and her profound modesty never left any room for complacency. She was oppressed by an abiding sense of the inequality of society. This is what gave her that severe outward aspect, so

[1] Einstein, *Ideas and Opinions*, op. cit., p. 227.

easily misinterpreted by those who were not close to her—a curious severity unrelieved by any artistic qualities.'[1]

The moral implications of scientific creativity are linked with its aesthetic implications. Einstein sought, in the writings of many thinkers, not logical arguments, but aesthetic impressions. Kant's arguments, for example, offered him nothing, but he liked to read Kant because the philosopher's language and mode of thinking were so characteristic of the heyday of German culture and the ideals—moral, in the first place—of German intellectuals of the age of Lessing and Kant. The connection between moral and aesthetic ideals is even more apparent when works of art are considered. In music, for example, Einstein preferred works expressive of the harmony of reality. To him Bach had an 'architectural' quality, reminiscent of the graceful, soaring lines of a Gothic cathedral and, at the same time, of a graceful system of logical conclusions. Wagner seemed too personal, too subjective. In Mozart, Einstein found humanity, refinement and, last but not least, humour. He once remarked that humour helped to 'mitigate the easily paralysing sense of responsibility' and was a 'consolation in the face of life's hardships'.

To Einstein art was a course of moral impulses. It could not remove 'life's hardships' or make one forget one's social responsibilities, but it made one's impressions and emotions bearable, directing them towards scientific interests and the search for that cosmic harmony which for Einstein was linked with moral harmony.

Here we must note an important difference between Einstein's attitude towards the search for 'extra-personal' harmony and Dostoyevsky's attitude. With Einstein, the 'extra-personal' was truly extra-personal: he became com-

[1] Ibid., pp. 77–8.

pletely oblivious of the self. To Einstein his own personality was an inconsequential thing and complete forgetfulness of it was a condition for scientific achievement.

Not so with Dostoyevsky. He never forgot about himself or his psychological conflicts. All of his characters are, to a greater or lesser degree, mouthpieces for his own reflections, emotions and recollections, which is why all of Dostoyevsky's novels are more or less autobiographical. When we take a closer look at Dostoyevsky's personality and its reflection in his work we see that Dostoyevsky constantly experimented not only on his heroes but on himself as well; every experiment on a hero was at the same time an experiment on himself. Whether it is Dostoyevsky himself or a trait of his personality which is represented in his hero, he is always isolated, compelled to resolve a problem in order to emerge from his intellectual or moral conflict (usually they are identical).

Dostoyevsky in this respect was quite unlike Tolstoy, who was extremely responsive to man's links with nature. One of his finest heroes, the old, cunning, powerful Yeroshka from *The Cossacks*, is as much at home on a river bank, in a forest, or on an animal trail as are the animals who have beaten that trail.

The setting of Dostoyevsky's plots is never natural. It is a fantastic visual accompaniment to the hero's moods and more especially to his thoughts. The harmony to which Dostoyevsky aspires is not a biological harmony, not a realisation of one's connections with nature. What he needs is a feeling of contact with people, a feeling of social harmony, a feeling that his *thoughts* are not self-contradictory but have a moral value.

The fact that, with Tolstoy, sensations come first did not prevent him from launching a rationalist critique of social reality. His sensualism coexists with his conviction of the irrationality and uselessness of practically every public

45

institution he considered. His criticism of the existing social system was a rationalist criticism which included, as with Rousseau, the concept of natural harmony. 'Natural' in the literal sense, since nature was the standard of perfect reality. People discover harmony when they come closer to nature, closer to the soil, which implies intimacy with the people who till it, and even more important, with the earth itself. Here Tolstoy's philosophy coincided with his poetics. His creative genius attained its greatest heights in scenes representing man in contact with nature or merging with nature, or the juxtaposition of the harmony of nature with the disharmony of society. An excellent illustration of this is the opening passage from *Resurrection*.

'Though hundreds of thousands had done their very best to disfigure the small piece of land on which they were crowded together, paving the land with stones, scraping away every sprouting blade of grass, lopping off the branches of trees, driving away birds and beasts, filling the air with the smoke of coal and oil—still, spring was spring, even in the town.

'The sun shone warm, the air was balmy, the grass, where it did not get scraped away, revived and sprang up everywhere: between the paving stones as well as on the narrow strips of lawn on the boulevards. The birches, the poplars, and the bird-cherry trees were unfolding their gummy and fragrant leaves, the swelling buds were bursting on the lime-trees; jackdaws, sparrows, and pigeons, filled with the joy of spring, were getting their nests ready; flies warmed by the sunshine were buzzing along the walls. All were glad: the plants, the birds, the insects, and the children. But men, grown-up men and women, did not leave off cheating and tormenting themselves and each other. It was not this spring morning they thought sacred and important, not the beauty of God's world, given for the benefit of all creatures—a beauty which inclines the heart to peace, harmony, and love—but only their own devices for getting the upper hand over each other.'[1]

Here is clearly expressed the basic, pivotal tendency of Tolstoy's poetics. Social harmony is a consequence of, or a part of, natural harmony; social disharmony develops because man is isolated from the natural harmony of the spring morning, the sun, the grass and the birds, and spurns 'the beauty of God's world'. The senselessness and disharmony of the big city is a consequence of the exclusion of nature. Yet nature triumphs and the feeling—feeling, not idea—of spring is represented with marvellous economy, depth and precision. Dostoyevsky, too, uses motifs of awakening nature, as in Karamazov's 'sticky little leaves', but how unlike Tolstoy's 'gummy and fragrant leaves' of the birches, the poplars and the bird-cherry trees they are. Far from representing man's kinship to nature, it expresses the hero's feelings. The 'sticky little leaves' are a symbol of useless affection for a disharmonised world. The harmony to which Dostoyevsky aspired was an internal, human, harmonious relationship among people.

With Dostoyevsky, man is separated from nature; this is his tragedy, the tragedy of the isolation of the individual. Indeed, Dostoyevsky's city scenes tend to stress man's isolation even in a crowd, amidst all the bustle of a city thoroughfare.

At this point, one might compare the attitudes of Tolstoy, Dostoyevsky and Einstein to the supreme isolation of death.

Thoughts of death are ever-present in Tolstoy; and he seeks refuge, either in Epicurus' dictum ('So long as we exist,

[1] Lev Tolstoy, *Resurrection*, translated by Louise Mandy (Foreign Languages Publishing House, Moscow), pp. 9–10.

death is not with us; but when death comes, then we do not exist') or in the even less convincing Biblical fairy-tale of resurrection. Tolstoy the artist could have been inspired by Schiller's words: 'You fear death? You dream of immortality? Live as a whole. Though you will die, it will continue eternally'—assuming the 'whole' to mean nature. In his story *Three Deaths*, Tolstoy compares the harmonious, peaceful end of a tree with the cruel, senseless death of people. He represents the tree's death as part of the eternal harmony of nature: 'Birds in the thickets sang joyfully in utter abandon, green leaves rustled serenely in the treetops, and the boughs of living trees swayed slowly over the drooping dead tree.'

Tolstoy has a story, *Master and Labourer*, in which a man sacrifices his life for another man. But there is no dissolving of the man in the human 'whole', in the immortal life of mankind.

Dostoyevsky, too, has no such 'dissolution', though he craves for it. His hero is alone among other men, and therein lies his tragedy. The hero either perishes or must endure sufferings worse than death in an effort to resolve, not personal, but general human moral problems. These experiments on himself and equally cruel experiments on others are designed to answer the question confronting mankind. In his conversation with Alyosha, Ivan Karamazov torments his brother and himself, and in his dialogue with the devil himself alone, in his efforts to resolve the problem of social existence; can social harmony be based on the neglect of a single human life? Such problems drive thoughts of death from the conscience of Dostoyevsky's heroes. The principal, dominating theme of their consciousness is thought, thought of a general human nature, and therefore immortal.

In Einstein's attitude towards death we find a certain

synthesis of Tolstoy's sense of kinship with nature and the absorption in human problems characteristic of Dostoyevsky. When a visitor once asked Einstein how he would judge his life on his death-bed, Einstein answered: 'I would not be interested in such a question, either on my death-bed or at any time. After all, I am only a tiny particle of nature.'[1]

He gave a similar answer in 1916, when he was seriously ill, to Hedwig Born (Max Born's wife), who asked him whether he feared death. 'No,' he said, 'I feel myself so much a part of everything living that I am not in the least concerned with the beginning or ending of the concrete existence of any person in this eternal flow.'[2]

This awareness is not only of the eternal flow of natural processes but also of the eternal flow of human knowledge and activity. When scientific curiosity is linked with the service of mankind, the scientist develops a logical understanding and an emotional realisation of the interrelation of the generations. In some cases this may precede scientific activity and to some extent determine it, as with Frédéric Joliot-Curie.

'Every man', he wrote, 'involuntarily shies away from the thought that beyond death there is no existence. The notion of a void has always been so unbearable to men that they have sought shelter in a belief in the life of the next world, received as a gift from God or from the gods. I am a rationalist by nature, and even as a callow youth I rejected this feeble and groundless faith. Many times have I witnessed the bitter desperation of people who have lost their faith. But . . . I would like to say this: Why the devil should life beyond the grave be in another world? Even as a youth when I thought of death I saw it as an essentially human and

[1] Helle Zeit—Dunkle Zeit, op. cit., S. 87.
[2] Ibid., S. 36.

earthly problem. Is not eternity a living, tangible sequence, connecting us with the things and people who have existed before us? If I may, I should like to share a memory with you.

'When I was a boy, I was busy doing my homework one evening when I happened to touch a tin candlestick, a family relic. I stopped writing, gripped by a sudden excitement. I closed my eyes and saw scenes that the old candlestick must have witnessed: someone going down to the cellar for a bottle of wine on a birthday, people sitting at night around a deceased member of the family. I seemed to feel the warmth of the hands that had held the candlestick over the centuries, I seemed to see their faces. I felt a tremendous support in the vanished multitude. It was a fantasy, of course, but the candlestick helped me to recall those who were with us no longer. I saw them alive, and I was finally rid of the fear of non-existence.

'Every man leaves an indelible trace on earth, whether it be in the wood of a banister or the stone step of a staircase. I like the wood, shiny from the contact of countless hands, the stone with depressions worn out by many feet, I like my old candlestick. Because they are Eternity.'[1]

The feeling of the relation between the generations is the first step in the transition from the personal to the 'extra-personal'. This *feeling* develops into an *understanding* of the irreversible evolution of mankind from chaos to harmony. Every person on earth contributes to this evolution, and this constitutes his real, earthly immortality.

For Dostoyevsky, as for Einstein, the problem of personal immortality was fused with the more general problem: does there exist a cosmic and moral harmony of the *extra-personal* based, not on the rejection of the personal, local, individual or microscopic, but on the apotheosis of the individual. We

[1] M. Rouze, *Frédéric Joliot-Curie* (Paris, 1950), p. 53–4.

shall be showing that the drama of Einstein and the infinitely more painful drama of Dostoyevsky are linked with this problem.

'The drama of Einstein' is an arbitrary notion. The fact that thirty-odd years of intense effort by a genius did not produce the unified field theory is, doubtless, a dramatic fact. But in all his searchings for the theory, Einstein never for one moment doubted its possibility in principle. He thought that a further generalisation of non-Euclidean geometry towards an even more non-Euclidean (in the sense of more paradoxical) geometry would lead to the goal. Even more confident was he of the existence of cosmic harmony.

Dostoyevsky's drama really was a drama, tragic and irreconcilable. He proceeded from a simple and traditional 'Euclidean' faith in providential harmony, allowed for a paradoxical 'non-Euclidean' harmony and, finding that it ignored individual fates, declared that the world was unknowable and returned to 'Euclidean' faith and official orthodoxy. This was the evolution of the thinker. The artist could not turn back, the logic of creative art was irreversible, and in his heart of hearts Dostoyevsky could not help being a 'rebel'.

It is now the moment to quote Ivan Karamazov's rejection of 'non-Euclidean' harmony. His first premise is that the human mind is endowed with an understanding of the three dimensions of space only. It is a 'Euclidean' mind. 'If God really exists and if he really has created the world, Ivan says, ' "then he created it in accordance with Euclidean geometry." ' This, however, turns out to be debatable:

' "And yet there have been and there still are mathematicians and philosophers, some of them indeed men of

Einstein and Dostoyevsky

extraordinary genius, who doubt whether the whole universe, or, to put it more widely, all existence, was created only according to Euclidean geometry. They even dare to dream that two parallel lines which, according to Euclid, can never meet on earth, may meet somewhere in infinity. I, my dear chap, have come to the conclusion that if I can't understand even that, then how can I be expected to understand God? I humbly admit that I have no aptitude for settling such questions. I have a Euclidean, an earthly mind. So how can I be expected to solve problems which are not of this world? I advise you, too, Alyosha, my friend, never to think about it, and least of all about whether there is a god or not. All these are problems which are entirely unsuited to a mind created with an understanding of only three dimensions." '[1]

But after refusing to consider 'non-Euclidean' problems and the question of the existence of God, Ivan reverts to the 'non-Euclidean' harmony (' "I believe in the eternal harmony into which we are all supposed to merge one day. I believe in the Word to which the universe is striving and which itself was 'with God' and which was God, and, well, so on and so forth, *ad infinitum*." ') He concedes its existence, though he refuses to accept it. A non-Euclidean harmony is not a moral harmony:

' "Let me put it another way: I'm convinced, like a child, that the wounds will heal and their traces will fade away, that all the offensive and comical spectacle of human contradictions will vanish like a pitiful mirage, like a horrible and odious invention of the feeble and infinitely puny Euclidean mind of man, and that in the world's finale, at the moment of eternal harmony, something so precious will happen that it will satisfy all hearts, that it will allay all bitter resentments, that it will atone for all men's crimes, all

[1] Dostoyevsky, *The Brother Karamazov*, op. cit., pp. 264–5.

the blood they have shed. It will suffice not only for the
forgiveness but also for the justification of everything that
ever happened to men. Well, let it. Let it all come to pass,
but I don't accept it." '[1]

Why does Ivan refuse to accept a 'non-Euclidean'
harmony? This question (and the whole of his conversation
with Alyosha) is examined in the concluding chapter of the
present book. Here we will note the 'macroscopic' failures
of the harmony; we shall consider its basic failure, the
ignoring of individual 'microscopic' fates, later on.

The 'macroscopic' failures of providential harmony are
stated in many of Dostoyevsky's books, and most pithily in
the devil's remarks to Ivan Karamazov. The first fault is the
static quality of this harmony. An eternal harmony without
irreversible evolution, an eternal state without individual
events—appears tedious and unreal. Consider a harmonious
scheme lacking events of any kind. Does such a harmony
really exist? Is it not a hollow and tedious fantasy?

Dostoyevsky draws an unusual and penetrating picture of
a tedious, spiritual eternity. In *Crime and Punishment* Svidrigaylov tells Raskolnikov:

' "We always imagine eternity as something beyond our
conception, something vast, vast! But why must it be vast?
Instead of all that, what if it's one little room, like a bath-
house in the country, black and grimy, with spiders in every
corner, and that's all eternity is? I sometimes fancy it is
like that." '[2]

The ghostliness of the country bath-house is of the same
nature as the ghostliness of Petersburg, which Dostoyevsky
stresses so much in his novels and stories. A whole in which

[1] Ibid., p. 265.
[2] Dostoyevsky, *Crime and Punishment*, translated by Constance Garnett
(Random House, 1956), p. 261.

the elements are ignored ceases to be real. Time and again Dostoyevsky speaks of the disintegration of the whole into disconnected, unimportant elements, and the ghostliness of such a whole. Here is a picture of Petersburg—as always, precise and specific, but a picture of disintegration, of mutual disregard and mutual indifference. In *The Raw Youth* the hero is walking in the city:

'It had become quite dark and the weather had changed; it was dry, but the Petersburg wind, sharp and biting, blew from behind me, sweeping up dust and sand. What a multitude of sullen faces as the common folk hurried back to their hiding places from the day's work! Each with his own sullen concern showing on his face, and probably not a single uniting thought in the whole crowd! Kraft is right: everyone is separate. I met a small boy, so small that it was surprising to see him all alone in the street at such an hour; he seemed to have lost his way. A woman stopped for a moment to talk with him, but, failing to make out what he wanted, shrugged her shoulders and went on, leaving him alone in the darkness.'

Again and again Dostoyevsky portrays such phantom cities, dream cities that may vanish all of a sudden. A community deprived of genuine harmony (one that is concerned with individual fates) is an immaterial place.

In *The Brothers Karamazov* we find a masterpiece of Dostoyevsky's characteristic style, vivid and precise. The picture is real and tangible, but suddenly becomes transparent, nebulous. The devil appears to Ivan Karamazov. Here is a phantom, which Ivan knows it a personification of his most agonised thoughts; but it is an extremely realistic phantom, which the reader also sees and may indeed find more realistic than many living characters.

'It was a gentleman, or rather a Russian gentleman of a

certain type, no longer young, *qui frisait la cinquantaine,* as the French say, with rather long, thick, dark hair, only just streaked with grey, and a small clipped, pointed beard. He was wearing a sort of brown coat, evidently cut by a good tailor, but becoming threadbare, made about three years before and quite out of fashion now, in a style that had not been worn for two years by well-to-do men about town. His linen and his long scarf-like cravat were such as were worn by gentlemen, but on closer inspection his linen appeared dirty and the wide scarf very threadbare. The visitor's check trousers were of an excellent cut, but again were a little too light in colour and a little too tight, and the same was true of his white fluffy felt hat, which was certainly not in fashion. In short, he gave the impression of a well-bred gentleman who was rather hard up.'[1]

This is no majestic spirit of evil. It is a very real image, like Svidrigaylov's bath-house, only even more common, commonplace and trite. This devil even tells Ivan how he caught a cold:

' "I was in a hurry just then to get to a diplomatic reception, given by a highly placed Petersburg lady, who was aiming at obtaining a ministerial post for her husband. Well, naturally, evening dress, white tie and tails, gloves, although I happened to be goodness knows where at the time and to get to earth I had to fly through space. . . . Of course, it was only a matter of a second, but then even a ray of light from the sun takes eight minutes to get to earth, and there I was—imagine it!—in evening dress and open waistcoat. Spirits do not freeze, but once you have assumed human form—anyway, I did a silly thing and set off, and, you know, in those empty spaces, in the ether, in the water that is above the firmament—why there's such a frost—you

[1] Dostoyevsky, *The Brothers Karamazov,* op. cit., p. 694.

55

can hardly call it a frost—just imagine, one hundred and fifty degrees below zero!'[1]

Now comes what explains, among other things, the mixture of triteness in the character and the cosmic scale of the eternal problem it expresses. The devil tells Ivan of his purpose, which is the negation of harmony. Without such negation everything disappears. 'If everything on earth were rational, nothing would happen.' There would be no 'events'.

' "I'm afraid," ' the devil tells Ivan, ' "you're determined to take me for some elderly Khlestakov, but my fate has been a far more tragic one. By some primordial decree, which I could never make out, I was appointed to negate, whereas, as a matter of fact, I'm genuinely kind-hearted and not at all good at 'negation'. 'No, no, you go and negate, for without negation there is no criticism, and what sort of journal is it that has no section for criticism? Without criticism there would be nothing but "hosannah". But "hosannah" alone is not enough for life. It is necessary for "hosannah" to be tried in the crucible of doubt', and so on in the same vein. Still, it is none of my business. I didn't create the world, and I am not answerable for it. They have chosen their scapegoat, made me contribute to the critical section and life is the result. And what a farce that is! I openly demand annihilation for myself. No, they say, you must live because there'd be nothing without you. If everything on earth were rational, nothing would happen. Without you, there would be no events, and it is imperative that there should be events. So ᵀ obey, grudgingly and introduce the irrational element. People take the farce seriously in spite of their undoubted intelligence. That is their tragedy. Of course, they suffer, but—they live. They

[1] Ibid., p. 699.

live a real, not an illusory life; for suffering is life. Without suffering, what pleasure would they derive from it? Everything would be transformed into an endless religious service: it would be holy, but a trifle dull." [1]

Thus reality appears when 'hosannah', i.e. the assertion of 'macroscopic' harmony, 'is tried in the crucible of doubt'. Otherwise everything would be 'an endless religious service', an endless holy tedium of illusory reality. The devil then raises the problem to the level of cosmology.

' "You're thinking of the earth: why, our present earth has probably repeated itself a billion times. I mean, it has become extinct, frozen, cracked, fallen to pieces, resolved itself into its component elements, become again the water above the firmament, then again a comet, again a sun, again an earth from the sun—this evolution, you see, has repeated itself an infinite number of times, and all in the same way, over and over again, down to the smallest detail. A most indecently tedious business . . ." [2]

Dostoyevsky presents two poles of a quasi-illusory existence, and neither is real without the other. At one pole are disintegrated individual lives without a unifying idea, without a common 'macroscopic' harmony. This is Petersburg in *The Raw Youth* (and not only there), a city whose ghostliness is due to the disintegration of the whole. At the other pole stands the harmony of the whole, deprived of the 'events' that alone are capable of altering the whole history of the universe and making it irreversible. The eternal recylcing and endless repetition is 'a most indecently tedious business', an illusory existence, in fact.

Where, then, is the true harmony, the true reality, the true life? Dostoyevsky intended us to find it in Alyosha

[1] Ibid., pp. 700–1.
[2] Ibid., p. 703.

Karamazov, Father Zossima and official orthodoxy, but his poetics threw the whole weight of his descriptive powers into the other scale. What he had intended to convey turns out to be creatively unconvincing. Dostoyevsky could find no prototypes for the supposed merging of individual existences with the 'music of the spheres', that is, with an evolutionary cosmos. The merger was illusory, even pathological.

In *The Idiot* Dostoyevsky describes moments of supreme harmony, moments in which the individual life appears to merge into the life of the whole—moments that precede an epileptic fit. Prince Myshkin 'remembered among other things that he always had such a moment, just before an epileptic fit (if it came on while he was awake). Suddenly, in the midst of sadness, spiritual darkness and oppression, there came a flash of light in his brain, and with extraordinary impetus all his vital forces began working at their highest tension. The sense of life, the consciousness of self, were multiplied ten times at these moments, which passed like a flash of lightning. When he was recovered again, he often told himself that these gleams and flashes of supreme sensation and self-awareness, which at the time seemed to be the highest form of existence, were nothing but disease, and an interruption, of the normal condition. If so, it was not the highest form of existence, but must be reckoned the lowest. He came at last to a paradoxical conclusion. 'What if it is disease?' he decided. 'What does it matter if it is abnormal, provided that the sensation, remembered and analysed afterwards in health, proves to be a pinnacle of harmony and beauty, an unimaginable awareness of completeness, of proportion, of reconciliation, of ecstatic devotion, in short, of the supreme synthesis of life?' . . . Since at that second, at the very last conscious moment before the fit, he had time to say to himself, clearly and consciously, 'Yes, for this moment one might give one's whole life!', then without doubt that moment was really worth the whole of life. He did not dwell on the dialectical part of his argument, however. Stupefaction, spiritual darkness, idiocy were the undeniable consequence of these 'higher moments'.[1]

Is there a *real* way to harmony that is neither illusory nor pathological? Dostoyevsky could not see it. But it does exist, and that is why Dostoyevsky's poetics is prophetic. So far we have been drawing parallels between Einstein's scientific creativity and Dostoyevsky's artistic creativity in an attempt to explain Einstein's statement: 'Dostoyevsky gives me more than any thinker, more than Gauss!' This remark cannot be explained completely. Dostoyevsky exerts his influence through certain moods which are not easily defined. As Einstein once remarked, it is difficult for a scientist to explain the psychological paths that lead to a discovery. After the discovery has been made it seems to be a simple record of objective events. That is why we have so far limited our task viewing Dostoyevsky through Einstein's eyes and Einstein through Dostoyevsky's. In this way certain traits of the two men stand out in bolder relief. Now our task is to draw parallels between the content of Dostoyevsky's artistic work and the content of Einstein's scientific work, compare their subsequent development, and trace this line of progress in contemporary science and contemporary life and, as far as possible, in the future.

[1] Dostoyevsky, *The Idiot*, translated by Constance Garnett (William Heinemann, London, 1946), pp. 219–20.

4
Thought and Action

We must now attempt to get to the root of the general themes that persist in Einstein's transition from physics to poetics. We must find what may be called 'the invariant of the transformation from Einstein to Dostoyevsky'. It cannot be found in his physics, for this would result in extremely superficial and formal analogies. The invariant is necessarily psychological, an inner dissatisfaction with the accepted scheme of cosmic and moral harmony. Einstein once made a remark which today appears highly significant. In a letter to Maurice Solovine, he wrote: 'The bodies we use for measuring objects react upon those objects.' From this follows a sudden sweeping conclusion, especially remarkable, coming as it does from a rationalist: 'Without sinning against reason we could never arrive at any conclusions.'[1]

In most cases the reaction of the measuring body upon the measured body in negligible. But suppose that the component particles of the bodies possess tremendous energy and that the measurement involves a violent, cataclysmic explosion. Suppose, too, that this is a case of a 'cruel experiment' that brings out the bodies' atomic structure. The reciprocal reactions of the measuring and measured bodies

[1] Einstein, *Lettres à Solovine*, op. cit., p. 129.

upon one another then become manifest, and extremely complex processes come into play, which break down the conventional scheme in which measuring rods have fixed dimensions and clocks have fixed rhythms. The result is an inevitable *sinning against reason* which reveals the fallacy of the macroscopic approach.

But what if the complex laws that have resulted in the release of these enormous quantities of energy are found to be fundamental? What if the macroscopic harmony can be derived from them?

This was what Einstein hoped for. His expectations did not materialise, however, and the investigation of the macroscopic harmony continued to require neglect of the atomic structure of bodies. Einstein considered this a defect of his relativity theory. In the *Autobiographical Notes* of 1949 he sums up his position as follows:

'First, a remark concerning the theory as it is characterised above. One is struck (by the fact) that the theory (except for four-dimensional space) introduces two kinds of physical things, i.e. (1) measuring rods and clocks, (2) all other things, e.g. the electromagnetic field, the material point, etc. This, in a certain sense, is inconsistent; strictly speaking measuring rods and clocks would have to be represented as solutions of the basic equations (objects consisting of moving atomic configurations), not, as it were, as theoretically self-sufficient entities.'[1]

Note that a 'cruel experiment' is 'cruel' by virtue of the fact that it transcends the confines of a *conventional* experiment, that it does not tolerate the conventional, '*sinful*' neglect of the more complex laws of reality. The hierarchy of these laws is endless, the complexity of reality is endless, and no single balanced logical system exhausts the complexity.

[1] Einstein, *Autobiographical Notes*, op. cit., p. 59.

Significantly enough, the first *physical* demonstration of the arbitrariness and restriction of a logical world scheme was suggested by the idea of *moral* harmony. This is seen in the atomic theory of Epicurus. Epicurus was troubled by the fatalism of a strictly mechanical world picture. If everything obeys natural laws that precisely determine every event, then man must submit to nature, and this is worse than religion: 'It were better to follow the myths about the gods', Epicurus wrote, 'than to become a slave to the destiny of the natural philosophers: for the former suggests a hope of placating the gods by worship, whereas the latter involves a necessity which knows no placation.'[1]

Absolute mechanical necessity is therefore modified by an inherent 'swerve' of atoms from their straight paths. Lucretius, in his exposition of Epicurus, says of man's relationship to nature:

'The mind feels some inner drive to do things, doing is not constrained like a conquered thing to bear and suffer. This is brought about by the tiny swerve of the first-beginnings in no determined direction of place and at no determined time.'[2]

Epicurus' brilliance consisted in combining two criteria of a physical theory, the moral and the physical, in one physical image. Ancient philosophy still retained its integrity and did not separate physical from moral criteria. The inherent 'swerve' does away with fatalism, and at the same time it explains how atoms gather together to form macroscopic bodies, that is, it explains the formation of the knowable world:

[1] Epicurus, letter to Menoeceus, *The Stoic and Epicurean Philosophers*, edited by W. J. Oates (Random House, New York, 1940).
[2] Titi Lucreti Cari *De Rerum Natura*, translation by Cyril Bailey (Clarendon Press, Oxford, 1947), p. 251.

'Herein I would fain that you should learn this too, that when first-bodies are being carried downwards straight through the void by their own weight, at times quite undetermined and at undetermined spots they push a little from their path: yet only just so much as you could call a change of trend. But if they were not used to swerve, all things would fall downwards through the deep void like drops of rain, nor could collision come to be, nor a blow brought to pass for the first-beginnings: so nature would never have brought ought to being.'[1]

The synthesis of moral and physical criteria does not mean the rejection of a purely objective description of reality. The point is that the sphere of *action* is the sphere of macroscopic bodies, and without macroscopic bodies nothing would be knowable.

Epicurus held atomic motions to be compounded of rectilinear displacements all taking place with the same velocity, 'swift as thought'. But how to account for the observed diversity of velocity in macroscopic bodies? According to Epicurus and Lucretius, the velocity of a macroscopic body is an average of the motions of the different atoms in different directions. Without the macroscopic processes, atoms could not be perceived and their reality would be incomplete. On the other hand, if there were no microscopic 'rebellion' against macroscopic existence, one could not speak of atoms as particles of macroscopic bodies. The bodies would simply be parts of space, to the detriment of their reality.

Here, as in ancient thinking in general, we find the germs of ideas and of contradictions that were to become explicit in much later times. We shall dwell on one such contradiction, that action must inevitably involve macroscopic objects.

[1] Ibid., pp. 247-9.

In Epicurus' physics paradoxical processes are possible which do not derive from the general logical scheme stating that bodies move in parallel paths. 'There are more things in heaven and earth, Horatio, than are dreamt of in your philosophy.' These are Hamlet's words and the juxta-position is not accidental. For Hamlet's tragedy consisted in his realisation of the complexity of existence. To act one must at some point put an end to the complicating of thought. 'Without sinning against reason we could never arrive at any conclusions.' Infinitely complicated thought cannot result in action; and the passing troops of Fortinbras, who do not stop to reflect on the complexities of the universe, serve as a mute reproach to reflective thought ('How all occasions do inform against me, and spur my dull revenge'). The illusory harmony was shattered on the terrace of Elsinore: 'The time is out of joint' . . . Hamlet erects a new harmony that calls for vengeance to be taken on his father's murderer. His thought, however, goes on and on, delaying its embodiment in action.

The possibility of such an embodiment is in principle, a proof of the congruity of thought and existence. Thought that cannot result in action lacks physical content; it is illusory and has no equivalent in reality. The Renaissance subscribed to the social and moral ideal of a harmony which was capable of realisation on earth. The scientific ideal of the Renaissance was a world system in which all basic concepts—the motions and interactions of bodies—could be verified experimentally. Experiment, physical and psychological, became the fundamental method of science.

Einstein completed the development of this classical ideal of science. He denied the physical reality of concepts that did not allow of experimental verification, of the testing of every hypothesis by observation. These unreal concepts include motion referred to a privileged system such as the ether, that is, absolute motion. They also include absolute simultaneity, absolute time, and absolute space. It is important to stress that only macroscopic experiments are involved. The very notion of experiment presupposes a macroscopic body which we refrain from analysing in such detail as to take its particulate structure into account. Otherwise, it would be impossible to measure experimentally the precise length of a line segment or the exact duration of a time interval, and the basis concepts of the world picture sought by classical science would lose their meaning.

Quantum mechanics represents a further development of the same idea. Reality remains knowable; the difference between the concept of a real body and the concept of a body we define as unreal is that the former is knowable *in principle*. It is wrong to suppose that an experiment alters the course of a process, as though the objective process were inseparable from the subjective act of cognition. Things happen independently of cognition. A process is knowable in principle by virtue of the fact that relatively macroscopic bodies take part in it. Later on, we shall see that even an individual particle may figure as such a body: its motion over a 'long' period of time (e.g. several thousandths of a second) is a macroscopic process compared with elementary ultra-microscopic processes lasting fractions of a nanosecond. If such macroscopic bodies take part in a process, we can in principle conceive of an experiment capable of detecting it. The experiment itself, as the solution of a cognitive problem, does not affect the phenomenon. Since the objective essence of a phenomenon includes interactions with macroscopic bodies, it can in principle be detected, it can in principle experience the action of the macroscopic process. This is the basis for the detection of the phenomenon. The exact values of the co-ordinates and velocity of a particle do not play hide-and-seek with the observer: they really do not exist, just as motion with reference to the ether is not merely elusive but really does not exist. The physical meaningless-ness of a concept derives from the absence of corresponding macroscopic objects in nature. In relativity theory, there is no absolute macroscopic body of reference—the ether; in quantum mechanics, there is no interacting macroscopic body in relation to which the position of a particle can be determined without simultaneously altering its momentum, or vice versa. The existence of *relative*, non-privileged bodies of reference and the existence of bodies of interaction that register *one* of several interconnected variables give physical meaning to the relativity theory and to quantum mechanics, respectively.

Niels Bohr was right when he objected to the phenomeno-logical interpretation of quantum mechanics, and to such expressions as: 'Observation disturbs the process' or 'Measurements create the physical attributes of objects'. An event is something which can in principle yield infor-mation, and measurement is in principle associated with the existence of a standard.[1]

Einstein's and Bohr's premise, according to which concepts that fail to offer a basis for conclusions capable of being verified by observation are physically meaningless, did more than yield the theory of relativity and provide the ground-work for quantum mechanics. Every epoch-making physical theory does more than just answer a current scientific question. The answer of a genius is always broader than the question. For the 'advance of reason', when new roads are being pursued, always involves an introspective advance as

[1] *Atomic Physics and Human Knowledge* (Moscow, 1961), p. 145–6.

well. The introspective advance of reason, i.e. the creation of new concepts and logical mathematical methods, means the eventual solution of new problems. The new methods of scientific research are in a way analogous to the poetics of artistic creation, which both solves and proposes more general creative tasks than those for whose purpose it was initially designed.

Let us note one feature of Einstein's and Bohr's 'poetics'. Their basic criterion is that mathematical and logical concepts are physically meaningful if their conclusions can in principle be experimentally verified. Their new concepts and methods referred to macroscopic constructions. Einstein's 'poetics' dealt with the macroscopic scale in the direct and conventional sense; Bohr's 'poetics' dealt with the motions of immutable, self-identical particles in domains substantially greater than the ultra-microscopic domains (in which it is impossible to act in terms of distinct objects). But Einstein's and Bohr's 'poetics' proved capable of posing, if not of solving, the more general problem of proceeding from the ultra-microscopic world to the macroscopic world.

The ultra-microscopic world is a world of energies, high even in comparison with those of relativity, that reveal the dependence of mass on velocity and other relationships of relativity theory, a world of infra-relativistic energies capable, not only of changing the world lines of particles but also of transforming particles of one type into another type.

Now let us return to the poetics of Dostoyevsky.

Epicurus' conclusion—that absolute conditioning of processes by rigid laws makes action meaningless and dooms one to fatalism—was congenial to Dostoyevsky. A belief in absolute and unalterable laws dooms man to inactivity. 'And what would the natural, logical fruit of consciousness be if not inertia, by which I mean consciously sitting with folded arms', Dostoyevsky writes in *Notes from Underground*.[1]

When the laws of nature are known, events appear to be independent of conscious activity: 'Therefore, all there is left to do is to discover these laws, and man will no longer be responsible for his acts. Life will be really easy for him then. All human acts will be listed in something like logarithm tables, say up to the number 108,000, and transferred to a time-table.'[2]

'Really easy for him' means the same as 'hopelessly difficult' with Epicurus. Dostoyevsky's 'ease' is, of course, ironical. He cannot accept fatalism:

'What do you say, folks, let's send all this reason to hell, just get all these logarithm tables out from under our feet and go back to our own stupid ways.'[3]

An entirely rational existence, lacking will or action, is illusory. 'Reason is only reason, and it only satisfies man's rational requirements. Desire, on the other hand, is the manifestation of life itself—the whole of life—and encompasses everything from reason down to scratching oneself. And although, when we're guided by our desires, life may often turn into a messy affair, it's still life and not a series of extractions of square roots.'[4]

Hence the incompatibility of activity and character, on the one hand, and knowledge, on the other: 'An intelligent man of the nineteenth century is bound to be a spineless creature, while the man of character, the man of action, is, in most cases, of limited intelligence.'[5]

[1] Dostoyevsky, *Notes from Underground*, translated by Andrew R. MacAndrew (Signet, 1961), p. 102.
[2] Ibid., p. 109.
[3] Ibid., pp. 109–10.
[4] Ibid., p. 112.
[5] Ibid., p. 92.

Knowledge erects a wall before man: 'The impossible, that is, a stone wall! What stone wall? Why, the laws of nature, of course: the conclusions of the natural sciences, of mathematics.'[1]

The solution is to ignore the laws that contradict moral intuition: 'But, good Lord, what do I care about the laws of nature and arithmetic if I have my reasons for disliking them, including the one about two and two making four!'[2]

This appears to be a stand based on moral intuition and irrationalism. But, it turns out, Dostoyevsky's poetics requires not so much the ignoring of natural laws and the logic of 'arithmetic' as a search for new laws and a new 'arithmetic'.

Remember that we are speaking of Dostoyevsky's *poetics*. The passages first quoted would never have become a landmark in the spiritual life of mankind had they not been confirmed and expanded by specific and authentic demonstrations of the behaviour of man under experimental conditions, by the author's barbarous interference in his hero's fate. What is more, the positive rationalism of Dostoyevsky's poetics stands in clear contrast to the negative irrationalism of his intellectual views. His is, first and foremost, a poetics of experiment. It is the poetics, not the intellectualism, that discredits the 'Euclidean nonsense' of a passive apperception of reality, discredits it with authentic concrete observations of man's behaviour in circumstances of 'cruel experiment'.

Dostoyevsky's experiments are mainly destructive and paradoxical, contradicting established systems. Their first victim is the providential harmony of the universe. The sum total of his observations disposes of providential harmony: 'The earth is saturated with tears from crust to centre.' A

[1] Ibid., p. 98.
[2] Ibid., p. 99.

more complex, 'non-Euclidean' harmony takes the stage. But a crueller experiment ('Would you agree to torture a single, tiny creature for the sake of such harmony?' Ivan Karamazov asks Alyosha) indicates that the more complex harmony is still arbitrary, since it ignores the fate of individuals.

A physical experiment can unleash energies which reveal the dependence of mass on velocity, when the relationships of relativity theory come into play. If carried further, the experiment may release ultra-relativistic energies, when it is no longer possible to regard the world line of particles as a basis for cosmic harmony and one must reckon with the discrete processes that constitute the world lines. In Dostoyevsky, the 'relativistic' experiments that destroy the traditional harmony are also followed by 'ultra-relativistic' experiments that destroy the 'macroscopic' harmony which ignores individual fates.

World harmony can never be based on tradition or intuition. It is verified by experiment, and not only its moral value is put to the test. In the work of Dostoyevsky, ignoring individual fates makes harmony illusory. On the other hand, individual fates, isolated from each other, enjoy an illusory existence. That is why, with Dostoyevsky, moral criteria develop into criteria of existence and acquire ontological meaning. This is the essence of Dostoyevsky's poetics. The image of a phantom city, being an *image*, is not a logical construction, but is produced by purely creative means.

The ontological nature of moral criteria in Dostoyevsky's poetics demonstrates that analogies between morality and physics are something more than analogies. Every poetic experiment, every clash between hero and circumstances is a test of the moral value, and indeed of the existence, of world harmony. But, as the experiment takes place in the realm of poetics, its result is not a logical formulation but an aesthetic impression of the illusory quality of existence.

With Dostoyevsky, poetics triumphs over logic and logical speculation, because it is a tool of experiment. Dostoyevsky experiments by manipulating the background, introducing new circumstances, making the heroes behave in different ways and putting words into their mouths. And all the time he is observing his heroes, waiting for the answer he is seeking, waiting to see the effect of a turn in the plot. The main purpose of Dostoyevsky's poetics is to achieve an inner authenticity. The selfsame criterion that is applied to scientific experiment holds for poetics. Dostoyevsky wrote of Edgar Allan Poe: 'He takes the most exceptional reality, places his hero in the most exceptional external or psychological circumstances and describes the state of the man's soul with remarkable powers of penetration and veracity.' Yet the most fantastic circumstances in Poe's work seem commonplace in comparison with those passages in Dostoyevsky where the most realistic setting—a documentary description of a Petersburg street, an inn or a garret—become a frame for a cosmic collision. And always the criteria of 'truth' and perception in depth are not so much aesthetic as ontological.

What then is the ontological result of an aesthetic experiment? A whole that disintegrates into individual processes and individual fates becomes unreal and illusory. But a whole, whose harmony is based on disregard for individual fates, is an 'endless religious service' without events, that is, equally illusory. Dostoyevsky's poetics creates a non-illusory existence in which individual fates constitute and give substance to the macroscopic harmony of reality.

5

Will Science Find Harmony in the Universe?

The notion that existence without harmony is an illusion or that harmony is only acquired by disregarding individual fates constitutes the link between the ethical problems in Dostoyevsky's books and the physical conclusions implicit in Einstein's theories. It is a link, not an analogy, a link between question and answer, where Dostoyevsky's *poetics* asks the question.

What physical idea can provide an answer to the onto-logical question posed in Dostoyevsky? It can be found in the fundamental characteristics of *physical* objects, as against their images, which lack physical reality. A real physical object is immutable and has identity. A body, as distinct from a volume of space, has identity, whereas one volume of space may differ in no way from another volume. Motion of a body is characterised by *non-trivial identity*, that is to say, a moving body does not lose its identity when the co-ordinates of its position change. A moving volume of space, on the other hand, is identified with any configuration it occupies, that is, it possesses no non-trivial identity. It is for this reason that Cartesian physics is unable to answer the basic question: how does a body differ from the space it moves in. It can ascribe no physical meaning to the image of a moving body. If substance and space are one and the same thing, if, as Descartes thought, a body is identical with the space it occupies, then nothing purely physical, nothing verifiable by observation, takes place when a body moves. Everything is reduced to a geometric conception. In this case the statement 'A given volume of space is *occupied* by a body' has no physical meaning; we cannot detect the difference between occupied space, that is, a body, and unoccupied space. When Descartes declared that his physics was geometry he was quite right, but this identification meant that physics lost its distinctive nature. It could no longer accord existential truth to two basic statements: 'A body *occupies* a given space' and 'A body *moves* in space'. Individualisation of the body, its separation from surrounding space, was the stumbling-block of Cartesian physics.

Opponents of Cartesian physics introduced qualities like mass or charge, designed to distinguish a body from surrounding space. But this involved a definition that was, strictly speaking, incompatible with the spatio-temporal localisation of a body. In order to estimate a body's mass, one must introduce other qualities, *all* of which have one feature in common: they have no physical meaning when the body is at rest. First of all, a body must have a certain velocity. Next, a certain acceleration. Then we must know what the body's acceleration will be in a given field of force. To be sure, we know how to determine velocity and acceleration *by reducing the path and going over to the limit*. But the concepts of instantaneous velocity and instantaneous acceleration have meaning only on the assumption that the body is moving. They describe, partially at least, a body's behaviour in moving from one place to another. They are not definitions

73

of spatial and temporal localisation. They are definitions of motion, of *change* in spatial and temporal localisation. Without such definitions, in relation to spatio-temporal localisation, the statement that a body *occupies* a certain space or is *located* in a certain place loses physical meaning.

Such problems become especially vivid when the question concerns particles, on the one hand, and the points at which they are located, on the other. The development of atomic theory reduced the problem of differentiating between a body and its location to that of differentiating between a particle and a point.

Imagine a *world* point, that is, four co-ordinates denoting a position in space and time. Imagine, further, a non-extended particle. What is the difference between the particle and the world point? What is an *event*, i.e. the occurence of the particle at the world point? When we consider a world line in itself, the questions take on a new form: 'What is the difference between real physical motion and a world line?' and 'What are the events that constitute a world line when it becomes a definition of a real particle?'

Developments in contemporary physics offer the possibility of new answers to these questions; or, rather, of outlining the contours of possible answers. A world harmony made up of world lines does not satisfy the requirement of physical meaningfulness. Whatever the world lines may be, however much we generalise, complicate and make paradoxical the geometrical relationships governing them, we can make them physically meaningful only by filling them with processes which are incompatible with displacement from one world point to another. If a particle's existence is reduced to its occurrence at a world point, and its motion, to a displacement from one point to another, then it is a geometrical point, not a physical particle. We can say *how* it moves, but we cannot assert that it is a real *particle*. We have, in fact, a sentence with a predicate but without a subject. There is no answer to the questions: *What* is moving? Whose motion is described by the world line?

Certain attempts at generalising modern theoretical physics select the transmutations of elementary particles as the events constituting a world line. A particle retains its identity from the macroscopic point of view, but when investigated in an ultra-microscopic approximation, it breaks down into a series of transmutations: a particle of one type changes into a particle of another type, which changes back into a particle of the initial type. Regenerations of this sort are said to constitute a physically real, occupied world line.

However, elementary regenerations *by themselves* have no physical meaning. What, in fact, is meant by the words 'a particle of a given type', 'a particle of a given type changes into a particle of another type', and 'the particle of the other type changes back into a particle of the initial type'? A particle's type, in terms of number of electrons, positrons, protons, etc., is determined by the shape of its world line, the curvature of this world line in a given field, and so on. In order to determine a particle's type one must establish *how* it moves, what its world line is and what its macroscopic behaviour is. (That is, behaviour that embraces many localised events.) Thus transmutation is a change in macroscopic behaviour, a change in world line. Without the concept of world line, particle regeneration is a physically meaningless concept, just as world line is, taken by itself, without the events that constitute it.

This is why it is wrong to imagine that the old conception of the motions of particles as elements of the world harmony is being replaced by a new conception of elementary transmutations. One must not assume that moving particles are being replaced by transmutable particles as the elementary bricks of the universe. Modern physics is approaching a more radical conclusion, that world harmony is not composed of elementary particles, since an 'elementary' process has meaning only in the context of the whole.

In this view the ultra-microscopic picture of elementary regenerations is physically meaningless; elementary re-generations are *virtual* processes that have physical meaning only when *eventual* world lines are considered. They are not motions of self-identical physical objects, but pairs of non-identical processes of the formation and annihilation of different, non-identical objects, to which even the concept of elementary particle is not applicable since this would imply a corresponding world line and corresponding macroscopic behaviour.

Can we, on these grounds, eliminate ultra-microscopic regenerations from the world picture? No, for in doing so, having escaped the Scylla of physically meaningless ultra-microscopic processes we should come to grief on the Charybdis of physically meaningless, unfilled, purely geo-metrical macroscopic world lines. It appears to be a question, not so much of elimination, as of abandoning the virtual ultra-microscopic processes, which are not susceptible of spatio-temporal representation, for macroscopic processes that at the same time do not ignore the ultra-microscopic elements.

The road is broadly indicated by Bohr's principle of complementarity. We can determine a particle's motion, its behaviour. Or, we can determine its spatio-temporal localisation, that is, its position in space and the time when it occupies that position. Suppose we have precisely deter-mined the spatio-temporal localisation of a particle. Then we cannot determine its behaviour at the corresponding world point with the same precision, we cannot judge the direction of the world line or the particle's momentum and energy: for these quantities we have to be satisfied with a wave definition. We record a certain wave-process, and according to its intensity, its amplitude, we judge of the *probability* of this or that magnitude of momentum and energy. Similarly, suppose we obtain a strictly corpuscular picture of a particle's energy and momentum, then we must accept a wave-picture of spatio-temporal localisation; we can determine the amplitude of the waves corresponding to the *probability* of encountering the particle at a world point. For the localisation of a particle in space and time is an operation that alters its behaviour. Conversely, determination of a particle's behaviour is an operation that changes its localisation.

Can this principle be generalised? Can analogical, or at least remotely similar, relationships be found outside quantum mechanics? Can, for instance, the principle of complementarity be applied to the problem of going over from any world of virtual, ultra-microscopic regenerations, lacking spatial existence, to a world of macroscopic world lines? For this transition is the road to cognition of the *real* harmony of existence. Bohr himself regarded the principle of complementarity as a broad, comprehensive logical principle which he illustrated with examples from widely different spheres of science and culture.

Suppose that every determination of a particle's position (*physical* determination, i.e. experimental verification of its presence at a given world point) is an operation that changes the eventual world line, the particle's eventual behaviour. It follows from this that every such determination causes a transmutation, in so far as a change in a particle's eventual

77

behaviour, a change in its eventual world line, means a change in the type the particle belongs to. Again, suppose that every determination of the particle's eventual behaviour (*physical* determination, i.e. experimental verification of its mass and charge, and of the other properties that distinguish one particle from another) is an operation that changes the particle's localisation in space and time. It follows from this that every transmutation is accompanied by a displacement in space and time. The result is the pattern of ultra-microscopic displacement-regenerations mentioned before which constitute the macroscopic world line and give it physical meaning. These are not displacements in the conventional sense: in a transmutation a particle does not move; it appears in another place at another moment. But we can treat this annihilation and reappearance as a displacement of a self-identical particle, a displacement of the selfsame particle.

This assumption enables one to derive from the ultra-microscopic picture of elementary regenerations the macroscopic relationships of the relativity theory. It enables one to identify the non-Euclidean harmony of the universe without ignoring elementary processes. But for this it is necessary to understand the concept of probability. If there is an even chance of a particle's displacement in a regeneration in any direction, then the probabilities of regeneration are symmetrical in space. After a great number of regeneration displacements, the particle will be near its initial position. Its macroscopic path will be almost zero, while its ultra-microscopic path, which includes all the individual elementary displacements, will be long. Now suppose there exists a slight dissymmetry in regeneration probability, that is, in one direction in space the probability of regeneration is greater than in the opposite direction. In that case, after a great number of regenerations, the particle will have moved in the direction of higher regeneration probability. The macroscopic path in that direction will be small if the dissymmetry of probabilities is small. Let the dissymmetry become very great. Then, evidently, the particle will be moving in the direction of more probable regenerations with a considerable macroscopic velocity and it will have a long macroscopic path. When we have a maximum dissymmetry of regeneration probabilities, that is to say, when the particle moves all the time in the same direction, the macroscopic path will be the same as the ultra-microscopic path, and the macroscopic velocity will be equal to the ultra-microscopic velocity, i.e. the velocity of light. This is the limiting velocity of a self-identical particle.

Now we can demonstrate that the propagation velocity of light is independent of the motion of the reference system. This statement can be derived from the ultra-microscopic picture of discrete space-time. First, note that the dissymmetry of regeneration probabilities can be identified with the momentum a particle receives in a field of force, and the propagation of the dissymmetry can be identified with field propagation. A particle's macroscopic velocity is different in systems moving relative to one another; it is proportional to the dissymetry of regeneration probabilities. In one system the particle will be found to be moving macroscopically fast, i.e. the displacements in one direction are much more frequent than in the other; in another system the particle is moving macroscopically slower, i.e. the number of displacements in one direction does not differ greatly from the number of displacements in the opposite direction. Thus all that changes is the macroscopic realisation of the dissymmetrical probability. As for the propagation of dissymmetry, it is the same in every regeneration, whether the dissymmetry is big or small, whether it is realised or not. Irrespective of how the dissymmetry is realised or in which direction the particle has moved on a given elementary segment, the vector of the dissymmetry of regeneration probability always points in the same direction. There is no spatial scattering to reduce the macroscopic velocity in comparison with the ultra-microscopic. The propagation of dissymmetry takes place with one and the same limiting velocity. In going over from one system to another which is moving in relation to it, the velocity of propagation of dissymmetry does not change unlike the magnitude of the dissymmetry and, hence, unlike the macroscopic velocity of a particle which is its realisation.

Clearly, we are here concerned with the ratio of the *probability* of an event to the *certainty* of the probability. If an event is merely probable, the probability itself has a certain quite definite value. An event consisting in the displacement of a particle in the direction in which it is pushed by a field is merely probable and does not take place on all elementary segments. But the probability of such a displacement (or, to be more precise, the difference between the probability of this displacement and of a displacement in the opposite direction, i.e. the dissymmetry of probabilities) exists on every segment. From this quantum condition it follows that the propagation of dissymmetry undergoes no spatial scattering and proceeds with a maximal, invariant velocity.

The greater a particle's momentum, the greater the dissymmetry of regeneration probabilities, and the closer the ultra-microscopic path approaches the macroscopic— in other words, the faster the particle travels—the greater *the extent to which the symmetry of elementary displacements* has been overcome. It is proportional to the particle's mass, which is thus dependent on the velocity. On what, then, does the fact that the initial symmetry of elementary displacements possesses a certain intensity depend? On what does the existence of mass in most elementary particles depend? This question can be linked with the fundamental problems of cosmology.

Contemporary cosmology allows for the existence of a finite, homogeneous metagalaxy. Its dimensions are so great that local non-homogeneities in the distribution of matter, such as accretions of matter in celestial bodies, galaxies and clusters of galaxies, are relatively very small. The metagalaxy acts upon a particle symmetrically, since it surrounds the particle on all sides with homogeneous matter of uniform thickness. Possibly this symmetrical action of the metagalaxy is responsible for the symmetry of a particle's random wanderings, while local fields, associated with local non-homogeneities in the distribution of matter, are responsible for dissymmetry, or for the overcoming of symmetry.

The considerations set forth here (a brief outline of what I have written elsewhere about ways and means of synthetising the ideas of Einstein and Bohr[1] may suggest, in general terms, that modern physics is working towards a scheme of world harmony that has room for ultra-microscopic, local processes. Classical physics proceeded from the premise that reality could be investigated by considering average quantities and quantitive relationships corresponding to observations in which the objects of observation were macroscopic, mass processes. Processes that were at variance with statistical laws were ignored, and therefore the theory did not take them into account. On this view, 'God is playing dice', that is the laws of reality leave individual events to chance. An individual throw of the dice, the fate of an individual molecule, has no effect whatsoever on the world

[1] B. Kuznetsov, *Einstein et Bohr*, 'Organon', No. 5, 1965.

harmony. After a great number of throws the distribution is found to satisfy the laws since each number comes up about as many times as any other. Taken in bulk, the molecules move according to the laws of thermodynamics; heat flows from the hotter body to the cooler; and the homogeneity of distribution of average molecule speeds increases.

But this statistical picture conceals the fundamental laws of mechanics, which determine not the probability of events and their mass results but the individual event. We know that the way in which a dice falls is precisely defined by its position at the moment it is thrown, the force with which it is thrown, the rotation it acquires, minute disturbances of the air, and a hundred and one other conditions that are quite specific. Equally, a molecule's behaviour is determined by its initial velocity and its interactions with neighbouring molecules. In the final analysis, the solutions of elementary processes are not left to chance.

Faced with the fact that the behaviour and position of a *single* particle was determined only statistically, and that quantum mechanics determined only the probability of an electron occurring at a given point, the probable time of its staying there and the probable magnitudes of its momentum and energy, some physicists none the less hoped that more precise laws would be found underlying this statistical picture. Others saw no hope of this and refused to accept quantum mechanics as equally valid with thermodynamics. Did they, then, consider statistical laws to be the 'ultimate' laws of nature? One can hardly claim, without serious reservations, that Niels Bohr ever thought in terms of 'ultimate' statistical laws. The enunciation of quantum mechanics, like the enunciation of the relativity theory, was an antidogmatic revolution that could not fail to undermine, if not destroy, the idea of 'ultimate' laws.

Einstein searched stubbornly for non-statistical 'sub-quantum' laws. But even he did not think in terms of 'hidden parameters' determining precisely an electron's position and momentum. He sought non-statistical laws of the micro-world, non-statistical in the sense that they would not ignore local events and leave them to chance. He sought, but could not find them.

To many it seemed that Einstein's 'grumbling' about quantum mechanics was prompted by the hope that, behind the scenes of quantum probability, science would discover a classically precise determinism of particle position and momentum. This, however, was not the case. Einstein did not assume that the relationships of indeterminacy concealed deeper classical relationships. True, the issue is an extremely complex one, but today Einstein's stand is viewed in a different light from ten or twenty years ago; we shall consider here only the aspect of the physical problem that can be linked, through analogy, with the ethical problem.

Einstein's social and moral ideals did not require that the statistical play of chance, with the individual as its victim, be replaced by a strict and precise definition of the individual's fate. It should not, of course, be assumed that his ideals had any influence on his physical theories. The question is not one of influence but of a certain ideological and psychological parallelism. It is worth recalling that Epicurus, appalled by the thought of fate having strict and precise power over people, introduced the concept of directionally random, microscopic displacement-swerves of particles from the paths decreed by physical laws. In those days moral ideals directly influenced physical systems. Nowadays such influence has been superseded by a degree of parallelism between scientific and moral ideals.

The world picture towards which modern physics is

moving remains a statistical picture, but not in the sense of neglecting individual processes. Macroscopic laws determine not only the probable outcome of individual processes; they give them physical meaning. We can take as an example the idea of momentum as representing a dissymmetry of displacement—regeneration probabilities, outlined above. It is a question of the dissymmetry of *probabilities*; the field determines the probability of the direction of a displacement. But the dissymmetry is constant on *every* separate, minimal segment, and on all segments without exception. This, in the final analysis, explains the invariance of the velocity of propagation of dissymmetry in passing from one frame of reference to another related frame.

On the other hand, ultra-microscopic processes do not obey macroscopic dissymmetry, but the scattering of ultra-microscopic displacements in various directions yields the moving particle's mass. These processes, expressing the symmetry of random wanderings, connect the micro-world with the homogeneous galaxy. In every case the ultra-microscopic processes give physical meaning to the scheme of world lines that constitutes the cosmic harmony.

A world line's fullness, that is, the existence of processes that cannot be reduced to changes in its shape, becomes physically observable at very high energies where we have the relativistic energies at which one must reckon with change in mass depending on change in the energy of a moving particle, and to the ultra-relativistic energies when physics enters the world of transmutational processes. When a particle is made to move at velocities comparable with that of light we have the physical equivalent of a 'cruel' experiment. When a particle is imparted energies that destroy its identity we have an 'ultra-cruel' experiment.

6

Dostoyevsky's Question and Einstein's Answer

At the end of the fourth book of *The Brothers Karamazov*, Dostoyevsky describes a meeting between Alyosha Karamazov and Captain Snegiryov, whom Dmitri Karamazov had offended shortly before. Alyosha offers Snegiryov money; Snegiryov dreams of climbing out of poverty, makes plans. Then there is a sudden change:

'Alyosha was about to embrace him, so pleased was he. But, glancing at him, he stopped short. Snegiryov stood with outstretched neck, protruding lips, and a frenzied, pale face, his lips moving as though he were going to say something; but no sound issued from them though he kept moving them. It was ghastly.

' "What's the matter?" asked Alyosha, with a sudden start.

' "You, Sir. I . . ." Snegiryov muttered, faltering and looking at him with a strange, wild, fixed stare, like a man who had made up his mind to throw himself down a precipice, and at the same time with a strange smile on his lips, "I, sir . . . you, sir . . . Would you like me to show you a

85

lovely trick, sir?" he suddenly said in a rapid, firm whisper, his speech no longer faltering." [1]

Snegiryov crumples the bills Alyosha has just given him, throws them down and tramples on them.

Shortly afterwards, Alyosha describes the scene to a friend of his. He explains to her why Snegiryov trampled on the money and why now he would surely accept it.

' ". . . He's worn out with suffering and he's very good-natured. I keep on wondering why he should suddenly have become so offended and trampled on the money." [2]

This, Alyosha goes on to say, was because Snegiryov was unable to conceal his delight at receiving the money.

' ". . . All the time he was talking to me his voice was so weak and feeble, and he spoke so fast, he kept chuckling in such a funny way, or he was crying—yes, he was crying, so delighted was he—and he talked about his daughters and—and the job he hoped to get in another town. . . . But no sooner had he poured out his heart than he felt ashamed of having opened up his heart like that to me. That's why he conceived such a hatred for me all at once." [3]

This narrative and its sequel exemplifies the concept of *rationalist poetics* in relation to Dostoyevsky's work. A paradoxical turn of mood becomes a natural and necessary development with the introduction of a paradoxical postulate: a restless, weak and timid soul fears exposure; this fear of revealing its weakness and confusion can only find outlet in a sudden transition from fawning gratitude to righteous, self-castigating pride. Of course, this is rationalist *poetics*: the paradoxical postulate is introduced not by a syllogism but by a specific detail of character (' "his voice was so weak and

[1] Dostoyevsky, *The Brothers Karamazov*, op. cit., pp. 237–8.
[2] Ibid., p. 242.
[3] Ibid., p. 242.

feeble, and he spoke so fast" '), that is, by a syllogism embodied in an image. Again, this is *rationalist* poetics, for the specific nature of the image is justified by Alyosha's desire to comprehend what has happened. He is interested not only in the conclusion that 'next time Snegiryov will accept the money' but also in the possibility of offering a rational explanation of an irrational scene.

This illustrates the most acute problem of rationalism. Every rationalist explanation depends on a certain curve in a man's behaviour. But is the personal, inimitable existence of the individual preserved in the process? Is not the individual ignored and reduced to the level of an obedient test animal whose fate is designed to confirm, demonstrate or illustrate a rationalist scheme? Alyosha's friend asks him:

' ". . . Listen, Alexey, don't you think our reasoning—I mean, yours—no, better say ours—don't you think it shows that we regard him—that unfortunate man—with contempt? I mean that we analyse his soul like this, as though from above? I mean that we're so absolutely certain that he'll accept the money. Don't you think so?" '[1]

To Dostoyevsky this is the crucial question. Later on Alyosha tells the girl:

' "Yes, Lise. You see, your asking whether we showed our contempt for that unhappy man by dissecting his soul was the question of a person who has suffered a lot. I'm afraid I don't know how to put it properly, but a person to whom such questions occur is himself capable of suffering. . . ." '[2]

Here is the crucial test. Can thought, freed from faith and tradition and pursuing its ideas to their conclusion escape the danger of disregarding a microscopic fate, and of transformating this fate into an insignificant detail in the macro-

[1] Dostoyevsky, *The Brothers Karamazov*, op. cit., p. 244.
[2] Ibid., pp. 245–6.

scopic harmony? Alyosha's answer is humble resignation: ' "Just think, what sort of contempt can it be if we ourselves are the same as he is, if everyone is like him" '[1] But the test has only just begun. Alyosha's conversation with Lise comes at the beginning of the fifth book of *The Brothers Karamazov*, which is entitled '*Pro and Contra*'. On the same day, Alyosha meets Ivan Karamazov and they talk about world harmony and the suffering of individual creatures.

The first argument that undermines world harmony is man's cruelty, his lust for tormenting helpless creatures. Snegiryov's agitation is explained, but can one accept his fate? Can one accept the fate of any innocent victim?

Ivan Karamazov illustrates his point by citing examples of torture, first of a horse, then of children:

' "Nekrassov has a poem about a peasant who flogs a horse about its eyes, 'its gentle eyes'. Who hasn't seen that? That is a truly Russian characteristic. He describes how a feeble nag, which has been pulling too heavy a cart, sticks in the mud. The peasant beats it, beats it savagely and, in the end, without realising why he is doing it, and intoxicated by the very act of beating, goes on showering heavy blows upon it. 'Weak as you are, pull you must! I don't care if you die so long as you go on pulling!' The nag pulls hard but without avail, and he begins lashing the poor defenceless creature across its weeping, 'gentle eyes'. Beside itself with pain, it gives one tremendous pull, pulls out the cart, and off it goes, trembling all over and gasping for breath, moving sideways, with a curious sort of skipping motion, unnaturally and shamefully—it's horrible in Nekrassov. But it's only a horse, and God has given us horses to be flogged. So the Tartars taught us, and left us the whip as a present. But men, too, can be flogged. An educated and well-brought-up gentleman

[1] Ibid., p. 244.

and his wife can birch their own little daughter, a child of seven—I have a full account of it. Daddy is glad that the twigs have knots, for, as he says, 'it will sting more', and so he begins 'stinging' his own daughter. I know for a fact that that there are people who get so excited that they derive a sensual pleasure from every blow, literally a sensual pleasure, which grows progressively with every subsequent blow. They beat for a minute, five minutes, ten minutes. The more it goes on, the more 'stinging' do the blows become. The child screams, at last it can scream no more, it is gasping for breath: 'Daddy, Daddy, dear Daddy!' " '[1]

These are no longer logical arguments. This gasping, choking 'Daddy, Daddy, dear Daddy!' drives logic out of the mind. To replace it with faith? No, faith is of no use here. The question is whether a logic can exist which will allow one to forget the cries of the tortured child? Dostoyevsky's poetics lead the conscience from the macroscopic harmony of the universe to the inimitable, individual fate of a separate creature. The concrete image opposes the logical scheme, and the reader is aware of an agonising torment of thought. Such poetic means serve, experimentally, like implements of torture. *Thought* is put to the test, it is subjected to crucial experiment.

Dostoyevsky enhances the tension by describing even more sadistic tortures:

' "A father and mother, 'most respectable people of high social position, of good education and breeding', hated their little five-year-old daughter. You see, I repeat most emphatically that this love of tormenting children, and only children, is a peculiar characteristic of a great many people. All other individuals of the human species these torturers treat benevolently and mildly like educated and humane

[1] Ibid., p. 271.

Europeans, but they are very fond of torturing children and, in a sense, this is their way of loving children. It's just the defencelessness of these little ones that tempts the torturers, the angelic trustfulness of the child, who has nowhere to go and no one to run to for protection—it is this that inflames the evil blood of the torturer. In every man, of course, a wild beast is hidden—the wild beast of irascibility, the wild beast of sensuous intoxication from the screams of a tortured victim, and the wild beast of diseases contracted in vice, gout, bad liver, and so on. This poor girl was subjected to every possible torture by those educated parents. They beat her, birched her, kicked her, without themselves knowing why, till her body was covered with bruises. At last they reached the height of refinement. They shut her up all night, in the cold and frost, in the privy. Because she didn't ask to get up at night (as though a child of five, sleeping its angelic sleep, could be trained at her age to ask for such a thing), they smeared her face with excrement and made her eat it, and it was her mother, her mother who made her! And that mother could sleep at night, after hearing the groans of the poor child locked up in that vile place! Do you realise what it means when a little creature like that, who's quite unable to understand what is happening to her, beats her little aching chest in that vile place, in the dark and cold, with her tiny fist and weeps searing, unresentful and gentle tears to 'dear, kind God' to protect her? Can you understand all this absurd and horrible business, my friend and brother, you meek and humble novice? Can you understand why all this absurd and horrible business is so necessary and has been brought to pass? They tell me that without it man could not even have existed on earth, for he would not have known good and evil. But why must we know good and evil when it costs so much? Why, the whole world of knowledge isn't worth that child's tears! I'm not talking of the sufferings of grown-up people, for they have eaten the apple, and to hell with them—let them all go to hell, but these little ones, these little ones! I'm sorry I'm torturing you, Alyosha. You're not yourself. I'll stop if you like." '[1]

Ivan describes an episode of a boy who had thrown a stone at a General's favourite hound:

' "They took him. They took him away from his mother, and he spent the night in the lock-up. Early next morning the General, in full dress, went out hunting. He mounted his horse, surrounded by his hangers-on, his whips, and his huntsmen, all mounted. His house serfs were all mustered to teach them a lesson, and in front of them all stood the child's mother. The boy was brought out of the lock-up. It was a bleak, cold misty autumn day, a perfect day for hunting. The General ordered the boy to be undressed. The little boy was stripped naked. He shivered, panic-stricken and not daring to utter a sound. 'Make him run!' ordered the General. 'Run, run!' the whips shouted at him. The boy ran. 'Catch him!' bawled the General, and set the whole pack of borzoi hounds on him. They hunted the child down before the eyes of his mother, and the hounds tore him to pieces! I believe the General was afterwards deprived of the right to administer his estates. Well, what was one to do with him? Shoot him? Shoot him for the satisfaction of our moral feelings? Tell me, Alyosha!"

' "Shoot him!" Alyosha said softly, raising his eyes to his brother with a pale, twisted sort of smile.

' "Bravo!" yelled Ivan with something like rapture. "If you say so, then—you're a fine hermit! So that's the sort of little demon dwelling in your heart, Alyosha Karamazov!"

' "What I said was absurd, but . . ."

[1] Ibid., pp. 271–2.

' ". . . The world is founded on absurdities and perhaps without them nothing would come to pass in it . . ." '[1]

' "What I said was absurd, but . . ." ' Alyosha says, and in response Ivan declares that the world is founded on absurdities. The 'absurdities' contradict the rational scheme but at the same time give it reality. Without them nothing would come to pass and the scheme would degenerate into a phantom. At the same time, these irrational 'absurdities' negate the rational scheme, they negate the harmony. These 'absurdities', these isolated facts that do not fit into the harmony, should not be ignored. Simply to understand the harmony, means suppressing the facts. ' "For if I should want to understand something I should instantly alter the facts," ' Ivan Karamazov says. In his determination not to alter them he rejects the rational harmony of existence, even the most paradoxical 'non-Euclidean' harmony.

First, the 'Euclidean' harmony goes, the simple, traditional scheme in which no one is to blame and everything is conditioned.

' ". . . Oh, all that my pitiful earthly Euclidean mind can grasp," ' Ivan Karamazov says, ' "is that suffering exists, and no one is to blame, that effect follows cause, simply and directly, that everything flows and finds its level—but then this is only Euclidean nonsense. I refuse to live by it! What do I care that no one is to blame that effects follows cause simply and directly, and that I know it—I must have retribution or I shall destroy myself . . ." '[2]

But the expiation or general reconciliation of non-Euclidean harmony are also of no use.

' ". . . I understand," ' Ivan goes on, ' "what a cataclysm of the universe it will be when everything in heaven and on

[1] Ibid., p. 273.
[2] Ibid., p. 274.

earth blends in one hymn of praise and everything that lives and has lived cries out: 'Thou art just, O Lord, for thy ways are revealed!' Then, indeed, the mother will embrace the torturer who has had her child torn to pieces by his dogs, and all three will cry aloud: 'Thou art just, O Lord!', and then, of course, the crown of knowledge will have been attained and everything will be explained. But here's the rub: I cannot accept it. While I'm on earth, I must fight against it. For, you see, Alyosha, if I live through such a moment, I shall perhaps myself cry aloud with the rest, as I look at the mother embracing her child's torturer: 'Thou art just, O Lord!' But I do not want to cry aloud then. While there's still time, I must arm myself against it, and that is why I renounce the higher harmony altogether. It is not worth one tear of that tortured girl who beat herself on the breast and prayed to her 'dear, kind Lord' in the stinking privy with her unexpiated tears! It is not worth it, because her tears remained unexpiated. They must be expiated, for otherwise there can be no harmony. But how, how are you to expiate them? Is it possible? Not, surely, by their being avenged? What do I want them avenged for? Why do I want hell for torturers? What good can hell do if their victims have already been tortured to death? . . ." [1]

No eventual harmony can expiate 'absurdities' that have already been committed. Hence, 'let even the parallel lines meet and let me see them meet. I shall see it, and I shall say that they've met, but still I won't accept it.'

Ivan poses to Alyosha the fundamental question of any harmony, 'Euclidean' or 'non-Euclidean'. This is the cruellest, test of rationalism. When Alyosha says that non-acceptance of the world is rebellion Ivan retorts:

' "Rebellion? I'm sorry to hear you say that," Ivan said

[1] Ibid., p. 275.

with feeling. "One can't go on living in a state of rebellion, and I want to live. Tell me, frankly—I appeal to you, answer me—imagine that it is you yourself who are devising human destiny with the aim of making men happy, of giving them peace and contentment at last, but that in doing so it is absolutely necessary to torture to death one tiny creature, the little girl who beat her breast with her little fist, and to found the edifice on her unavenged tears—would you consent to be the architect on those conditions? Tell me, and do not lie!"

' "No, I wouldn't," Alyosha said softly.'[1]

Raskolnikov asked himself the same question. For this is the cardinal test of any rational scheme of the universe. In *Crime and Punishment* the question is posed in a light which reveals its 'anti-statistical' nature. Raskolnikov sees a drunken fallen girl and thinks of her future. Her fate is hospital, wine, taverns, hospital again and an early death. And Raskolnikov says, sarcastically, of statistics:

' ". . . Ugh! But what does it matter? That's as it should be, they tell us. A certain percentage, they tell us, must every year go . . . that way . . . to the devil, I suppose, so that the rest may remain chaste, and not be interfered with. A percentage! What splendid words they have; they are so scientific, so consolatory. Once you've said 'percentage', there's nothing more to worry about. If we had any other word—maybe we might feel more uneasy . . ." '[2]

Did Dostoyevsky think in terms of the *complementarity* of a local, individual, inimitable existence, on the one hand, and the rational, general scheme of the world harmony, on the other? In other words, did he contemplate a harmony that would not ignore individual fates, and individual fates that

[1] Ibid., p. 276.
[2] Dostoyevsky, *Crime and Punishment*, op. cit., p. 47.

would be consistent with the eventual harmony of the whole? He did, but it remained a vague idea, unexpressed in any positive social and moral programme. Dostoyevsky's work is an unresolved question addressed to the future. Dostoyevsky saw the individual as a vehicle for the harmony of the whole, but his ideas were too insubstantial to be expressed in concrete images. He had plans to write a sequel to *The Brothers Karamazov*—reflecting on Alyosha's future, he saw him as a revolutionary, an idealised Karamazov—but he had drifted too close to Pobedonostsev and Katkov for the idea to materialise, even if death had allowed him to make the attempt.

Even his negative formula—that the individual causes a 'chain reaction' which destroys the whole—did not find creative images as concrete as his purely 'questioning' ones. The hero of Dostoyevsky's story, *The Dream of a Ridiculous Man*, continually loses his 'world line', and life becomes a purely individual process. The disintegration of the 'world line' is presented most vividly. The hero's statement, 'I suddenly felt that it really made no difference to me whether or not the world existed', is followed by a concrete picture of disintegration. A little girl runs up to him, entreating his help, but he merely shouts at her. He is indifferent to the girl's fate, as he is to everyone else's.

'The street was quite deserted. At a distance, a cabman was asleep on his box. The little girl was about eight. She had a scarf tied round her head and wore a ragged overcoat. She was all wet from the damp, but what struck me especially were her battered, wet shoes. I remember them to this day. She started tugging at my elbow, trying to make me pay attention to her. She wasn't crying, but she was spasmodically shouting some indistinct words which she couldn't pronounce too clearly, as she was shivering with cold. Something must have frightened her, for she kept repeating, "Mummy, Mummy!" and there was terror in her voice.

'I just glanced at her and, without saying a word, started walking away. She ran after me, tugging at my sleeve, I discerned a note in her voice that indicates despair in badly frightened children. I know that note well. And, although she spoke indistinctly, I gathered that her mother was dying somewhere, or that something had happened to her, and she'd rushed out to get help. But I wouldn't follow her. In fact, I decided to chase her away. I started telling her to go and find a policeman, but she clasped her little hands together and trotted along at my side, sobbing, trying to catch her breath. Finally I stamped my foot and shouted at her.'[1]

Later on the hero dreams that he is on a remote planet where moral harmony reigns and that he corrupts its inhabitants:

'Yes, in the end I corrupted the lot of them! How I managed to do, I can't say; I don't remember too clearly. My dream flashed through aeons, leaving only a general impression of the whole. All I know is that I caused their fall from grace. Like a sinister parasite, like a plague germ infecting whole kingdoms, I contaminated with my person that entire happy, sinless planet. They learned how to lie, they came to love it, they appreciated the beauty of untruth. It may have started with a joke, innocently, playfully, with a flirtation, but the germ of the lie penetrated their hearts, and they took a fancy to it.'[2]

The story ends in a positive 'chain reaction'. The hero is cured of indifference to the world, and his existence becomes

---

[1] Dostoyevsky, *The Dream of a Ridiculous Man*, in Dostoyevsky, *Notes from Underground*, op. cit., p. 207.
[2] Ibid., p. 220.

the initial point for its transformation. However, the negative and positive variants of an individual real, replete fate turned towards integral harmony, is abstract and not characteristic of Dostoyevsky's poetics. These only pose the *question* of an individual fate that is of consequence to the 'world line', and cannot be disregarded.

In one of his science-fiction stories Ray Bradbury describes how travellers into the past hunt a Tertiary monster. One of them *accidentally alters the fate* of some minor organisms, and as a result the earth evolves in a different way. When the travellers return to the present they find a changed world. A different candidate unexpectedly wins a presidential election, and the country is threatened with fascism. A single minor fact, unimportant to the statistical conception of reality, macroscopically undetectable and therefore apparently lacking physical existence, alters the world line of the whole; it becomes definable by virtue of the alteration, and therefore appears as real and essential for the whole.

A single biological or mechanical event is unable to alter the destinies of mankind, but they may to a greater or lesser extent be altered by a single human life, provided that the man's aspirations follow the macroscopic 'world line'. Such aspirations and their realisation constitute the world line, which is no mere formula but a history of people. At the same time, it is when individual fates embody aspirations for some macroscopic evolution of mankind that they acquire tangibility, real existence and macroscopic importance.

Dostoyevsky failed to show us this with the concreteness characteristic of his genius. This was the result of influences exerted by his character and environment on his poetics. Poetics are responsible for the internal logic of a work, which is frequently quite independent of the writer's intention. One's character, in turn, affects one's poetics. This 'uncontrollable interaction' of two aspects of creative art is an expression of a very deep and general complementarity of two components of creativity: abstract rationalism, and specific imagery and poetics. Taken in isolation, each component loses meaning and in effect ceases to exist. Abstract logical construction, when they are divorced from concrete, individual fates, become thoughts about nothing, a set of predicates without a subject. A concrete image divorced from the 'world line', from the ultimate macroscopic essence, is incapable of conveying real features (which are an expression of the links between the individual and the whole, of the importance of the individual for the whole) and thus loses meaning, becomes a subject without a predicate.

In Dostoyevsky's work we find a synthesis—incomplete and therefore tragic—of two trends of thought. They can, somewhat arbitrarily, be associated with the names of Newton and Goethe. The great poet and naturalist turned away from Newton, accusing the creator of classical science of abstract schematism that deprived nature of its colours. This did not prevent Goethe from himself creating a great rationalist poem.

Like Goethe, like any other great artist, Dostoyevsky *saw* the world with all the pores of his skin, and the concrete visible world was infinitely dear to him. Recall the 'sticky little leaves' at the very beginning of Ivan and Alyosha Karamazov's talk.

' "... I want to live and I go on living, even if it's against logic. However much I may disbelieve in the order of things, I still love the sticky little leaves that open up in the spring. I love the blue sky; I love some people, whom, you know, one loves sometimes without knowing why; I love great human achievements, in which I've perhaps lost faith long ago, but which from old habit my heart still reveres. (Here's your fish soup. Eat it. It's excellent. They know how to make it here.) I want to travel in Europe, Alyosha, and I shall be going abroad. I know very well that I'm only going to a graveyard, but it's a precious graveyard—yes, indeed! Precious are the dead that lie there. Every stone over them speaks of such an ardent life, of such a passionate faith in their achievements, their truth and their struggles that I know beforehand that I shall fall on the ground and kiss those stones and weep over them and—and at the same time I shall be deeply convinced that it's long been a graveyard and nothing more. And I shall not weep from despair, but simply because I shall be happy in my tears. I shall get drunk on my own emotion. I love the sticky little leaves of spring and the blue sky—yes I do! It's not a matter of intellect or logic. You love it all with your inside, with your belly. You love to feel your youthful powers asserting themselves for the first time . . ." '[1]

The 'sticky little leaves' do not fit into the logical pattern, but they draw Dostoyevsky's eyes and heart. Europe seems to him a graveyard, but he loves it with the same love as he has for everything that exists, even for what is allegorical: brave deeds, Man, the blue sky, 'the sticky little leaves of spring'.

Is it possible to devise a logic which has room for 'sticky little leaves' so that they lose their allegorical qualities? Is a universal harmony possible in which individuals will not be 'negligibles', in which individual fates will not be ignored? Is a rational poetics possible in which the logic of the universe is revealed through specific, poetic imagery?

These questions are uniquely interconnected. Firstly, if there is a logic that justifies the 'sticky little leaves', then

[1] Dostoyevsky, *The Brothers Karamazov*, op. cit., pp. 259–60.

there must be a universal harmony and a rational poetics. Secondly, and more important, our century has answered all three questions in the affirmative. We have developed a logic that does not ignore the individual but, on the contrary, adopts a loving attitude towards every detail of the universe. We are conscious of a moral harmony of the whole that does not ignore personal fates but, on the contrary, presupposes their apotheosis, their importance, their value. And we have identified real embodiments of rational poetics.

Today, as never before, the destinies of civilisation hang on the answer to the question: will mankind achieve moral harmony, will mankind find moral harmony in nature without ignoring the life and happiness of every man?

Let us consider the *real interactions* between the search for cosmic harmony in nature and the search for social and moral harmony. The search for cosmic harmony brought science into the world of relativity. At the dawn of the atomic age Frédéric Joliot-Curie discovered the chain reaction of nuclear fission, and his thoughts turned to the moral and social aspects of the newly emergent science of nuclear physics. In 1951 he recalled a talk he had had with Halban and Kowarski in 1939.

'We had just found the solution of one of the major problems of science, the chain reaction of atomic fission. We wondered what applications the discovery would have, what its consequences would be for mankind, and what we ourselves should now do. Should we go ahead, or halt and wait until the emergence of conditions capable of precluding any possibility of directing these important discoveries to an evil purpose. We decided that we must carry on our researches. We had to continue, for to sit with folded arms would mean to display cowardice and lack of confidence in the people.

'Our duty as scientists compelled us to continue the struggle to wrest from nature her secrets, which held the promise of great boons for mankind in the future. But at the same time we had to make the decision to enter the arena of public activity so as to ensure, together with the people, only peaceful use was made of our discovery.'

At the time it was not yet a question of the hydrogen bomb. Hiroshima lay in the future. Joliot, Halban and Kowarski could envisage uranium fission as a destructive force, but not such as to constitute a threat to civilisation. The problem was a moral one in itself. It generalised Raskolnikov's and Ivan Karamazov's problem: does future harmony justify the suffering and death of people? Only here the question was not acceptance or non-acceptance of the cosmic harmony. It was a matter of seeking its physical substratum. In these circumstance, 'opting out' would mean refusal to work for the advance of nuclear physics.

It was still a long way to Hiroshima, but not so long as to prevent a scientist's mind from weighing the real dangers. Voices were already being raised about the unpredictably destructive force of the newly discovered reactions. It was no longer possible to think in terms of trivial destruction. It was a matter of chain reaction: once initiated the catastrophe might expand in geometric progression.

After Hiroshima, the scientist's sense of social responsibility became more acute. Since the development of the hydrogen bomb it has become impossible for the scientist to work on the fundamental problems of the universe without at the same time facing social and moral problems. Today man's conscience is inseparable from his growing power over nature and his knowledge of its laws. In 1959 Robert Oppenheimer remarked that dulled consciences during the Second World War were the cause of great moral and political damage. Compunction, a sense of responsibility for every human life, must accompany scientific progress.

The search for cosmic harmony is currently progressing through the investigation of relativistic and ultra-relativistic energies. Cosmic harmony is not merely a scheme of world lines: it includes the ultra-microscopic processes of trans-mutation of elementary particles. The search for a theory of elementary particles that would include the laws of their transmutations could well lead, along with theoretical results (and maybe even before them), to a new expansion of usable energy resources, to the control of processes involving the output of ultra-relativistic energies.

This prospect is associated with Einstein's name. Already in the first quarter of the century, when Einstein's name was a symbol of theoretical thinking, remote from the problems of practical life, the widespread interest in the theory of relativity was an expression of intuitive confidence in the inevitability of far-reaching changes in human destinies which the practical implementation of the theory involved.

The application of the new forces of energy is linked with total automation of production on the basis of electronics and cybernetics. Electronic computers are used to automate information-collecting and control processes. When the new energies are employed in basic industrial processes, cybernetic automation (including the automated search for the best techniques and designs, and their automated introduction) will turn all industry into an automatically operating and automatically reconstructing mechanism.

A condition for the attainment of this standard of production will be the eradication of hostile labour relations and the introduction of a harmonious social system. The new system in industry will alter the content of human labour. In conventional automation, labour is increasingly restricted to the introduction of changes and improvements in an established technology. In cybernetically automated production, where the introduction of such changes will take place automatically, labour will be further restricted to the search for new physico-technical *principles* of an increasingly general and fundamental nature. These principles are physico-technical and, at the same time, technico-economic. Cybernetics makes it possible to automate technico-economic computations, and to use electronic computers to determine an optimal balance of industrial output, optimal geographic location of enterprises and optimal transportation routes. Here, as everywhere, cybernetics does not restrict but expands (or rather *elevates*) the sphere of conscious activity, the sphere that is left to man.

Will all this introduce any new features into the problem of moral harmony? We can with full justification call this *Dostoyevsky's question*. Many thinkers have formulated the problem of moral harmony more consistently and precisely than Dostoyevsky, but no one has set it forth in such tragic, paradoxical, and at the same time authentic scenes. After Dostoyevsky, moral harmony can no longer remain a theoretical problem. It has left its mark on the very soul of man. Nowadays no one would dare to plan a general harmony which disregarded individual fates.

'Where can the conditions be found for moral harmony?' is Dostoyevsky's question. Does the prospect of utilising relativistic and ultra-relativistic energies, the prospect of embodying and applying Einstein's ideas, provide an answer to it? Scientific and technical progress is capable of doing away with poverty and providing men with their essential requirements and comforts. Is mankind to be content with this? A harmonious society will demand a steady rise in the *level* of its requirements. This demand and its satisfaction are linked with the nature of labour, with the elimination of the difference between labour and science, with the shifting of the centre of activity to more fundamental physico-technical and technico-economic questions. And these are linked with a rise in emotional and moral potential, without which science and labour cannot progress.

These and similar developments are, in essence, synonymous with freedom. They free man's thinking from the shackles of tradition, from restraints dependent on traditional, established principles. Such continuous liberation is a basic prerequisite for, and a basic result of, scientific and technological progress in a harmonious society. It leads people away from the alternative of 'daily bread *or* freedom' which Dostoyevsky expresses through the mouth of the Grand Inquisitor in Ivan Karamazov's 'poem'. It tells how, some time early in the sixteenth century, Christ comes to Seville. He walks through the squares. The populace recognise and follow him. Not far from the parvis of the cathedral, he meets the Grand Inquisitor, a nonagenarian fanatic of Catholicism, who orders him to be taken away to a dark prison cell. At night the Inquisitor comes to Christ and sets forth his *profession de foi*. He reminds Christ of the three temptations posed to him in the wilderness, and of how he had refused to turn the stones of the desert into loaves, saying that man did not live by bread alone. The Inquisitor declares that for fifteen centuries the Church has been striving to do what Christ had refused to do, giving people bread, turning them into obedient slaves of the Church and depriving them of freedom. Then comes a turn of the argument, in the spirit of Pobedonostsev or Katkov: the Inquisitor's idea of 'bread at the cost of freedom' is linked with revolutionary ideas.

' "Decide for yourself who was right—you or he who questioned you then? Call to your mind the first question;

its meaning, though not in these words, was this: 'You want
to go into the world and you are going empty-handed, with
some promise of freedom, which men in their simplicity and
their innate lawlessness cannot even comprehend, which
they fear and dread—for nothing has ever been more un-
endurable to man and to human society than freedom!
And do you see the stones in this parched and barren desert?
Turn them into loaves, and mankind will run after you like a
flock of sheep, grateful and obedient, though forever
trembling with fear that you might withdraw your hand
and they would no longer have your loaves.' But you did
not want to deprive man of freedom and rejected the offer,
for, you thought, what sort of freedom is it if obedience is
bought with loaves of bread? You replied that man does not
live by bread alone, but do you know that for the sake of that
earthly bread the spirit of the earth will rise up against you
and will join battle with you and conquer you, and all will
follow him, crying 'Who is like this beast? He has given us
fire from heaven!' Do you know that ages will pass, and mankind will proclaim in its wisdom and science that there is no
crime and, therefore, no sin, but that there are only hungry
people. 'Feed them first, and then demand virtue of them!'—
that is what they will inscribe on the banner which they will
raise against you and which will destroy your temple . . ." '[1]

The Inquisitor goes on to say that a new Tower of Babel
will rise in place of Christ's temple, and that people will
come back to the Church, which alone can feed them,
contrary to the destructive 'not by bread alone'.

' "No . . . No science," he says, "will give them the bread
so long as they remain free. But in the end they will lay their
freedom at our feet . . ." '[2]

[1] Dostoyevsky, *The Brothers Karamazov*, op. cit., p. 283.
[2] Ibid., p. 284.

Of course, the idea of 'bread in place of freedom' unites the Grand Inquisitor, not with revolutionary ideas, but with authoritarian ideas that have nothing in common with socialism and are essentially hostile to socialism. Our interest, however, is not in the justly forgotten reactionary but in Dostoyevsky's *question*. Moral harmony requires that individual fates should not be crushed by an authoritarian machine, acting in the name of daily bread and offering men this bread at the price of their freedom. Can science provide *free* people with bread? This is another aspect of the basic collision: individual existence, and a statistical, authoritarian, universal harmony that ignores individual fates. The solution is seen today in a different light. Modern science draws a picture of the world in which cosmic processes are inseparable, physically, from ultra-microscopic processes. The application of modern science is connected with the flowering of individual existence, with the liberation of man's thought and activity from traditional limitations, with the transition to more fundamental problems and principles as the object of his consideration. We see here another 'isomorphism', another analogy, between modern science and the social, intellectual and moral effects of its applications. Modern science cannot treat ultra-microscopic processes as real without introducing macroscopic concepts, without defining a particle's macroscopic behaviour. Modern notions of moral harmony require that an individual existence be determined by its importance to the collective destiny. Only by acting on the destiny of a large collective can an individual existence acquire content, or social and moral meaning.

*   *   *

Thus, the physical, physico-technical, social and moral ideas of the twentieth century give a positive answer to the question posed by the nineteenth century. Let us repeat the basic expressions of the 'Dostoyevsky' question? We have found it in his poetics, in his 'cruel experimenting', in the paradoxicality and, at the same time, musicality of his plot development, in his language, wholly subordinated to morbid, feverish searchings for cosmic and moral harmony, in the settings that always stress and accentuate moral collisions.

This question could not merely be posed logically, it had to be embodied in artistic form. Dostoyevsky's poetics are thus a necessary component of the general question of the nineteenth century and linked with most of the important scientific, social and aesthetic ideas of the century.

The nineteenth century carried out the task imposed on it by the eighteenth century, the century of Reason. Rationalism developed rational science and an industry which laid aside empirical tradition and turned largely to applied natural science. But the earth continued to be 'saturated with human tears from crust to centre'. Millions of local tragedies were enacted on it. The death, poverty and loneliness of insulted and injured people represented the statistically trivial price of general macroscopic harmony.

The search for a new social harmony and improved conditions of life in a society which concerned itself with individual people was being conducted along lines incomprehensible to Dostoyevsky. This search, however, had to include a creative component. There had to appear (and survive) in nineteenth-century culture the *image* of the lonely, insulted, defeated human being, ignored by the macroscopic scheme of existence. It had to be an image, not a concept, for only an image can convey the inimitable, individual qualities of people, and this is the concern of poetics, not of logic, confronting the mind with the specific picture of an individual. Such collisions occur in the 'turning-point' scenes of Dostoyevsky's books, the critical moments at which the torment of thought seeking a rational harmony in the world can be seen through the realistic fabric. Such confrontations give reality to the rational harmony.

The collision between macroscopic harmony and local, microscopic (or ultra-microscopic) verification grew in physics, too. The theory of relativity sees the scheme of world lines as the basis of world harmony. But these lines only become real physical processes when they are filled with micro-process, which causes a transition from a world line characteristic of one type of particle to a world line characteristic of another type.

In the scientific and social effects of the advance and application of modern physics, we once again meet the problem of macroscopic harmony and individual fates. Science promises men a tremendous expansion of power resources, with the application of the new forms of energy. This expansion, coupled with cybernetic automation, will enable men to concentrate on the solution of more general and fundamental problems. This needs a keen conscience, a feeling of responsibility for the fate of every single human being. This feeling, so intense in Einstein, stems in part from the gallery of suffering characters that Dostoyevsky introduced to world culture.

Index

Index

Index